LIGHT & VIBRATION

LIGHT &
VIBRATION

CONSCIOUSNESS, MYSTICISM
& THE CULMINATION OF YOGA

SWAMI SIVANANDA RADHA

 timeless books 2016

timeless books
www.timeless.org

© 2016 timeless books

In Canada:
Box 9, Kootenay Bay, BC   V0B 1X0
contact@timeless.org
(800) 661-8711

In the United States:
P.O. Box 3543, Spokane, WA   99220-3543
info@timeless.org
(800) 251-9273

Design by Todd Stewart

ISBN 13: 978-1-932018-15-8

Library and Archives Canada Cataloguing in Publication

Radha, Swami Sivananda, 1911-1995.
    Light & vibration : consciousness, mysticism & the
culmination of yoga / Swami Sivananda Radha.

ISBN 978-1-932018-15-8

1. Yoga. 2. Saivism. I. Title.

BL1237.32.R34 2007   294.5'ttt436   C2007-901448-8

Printed in Canada
Interior: FSC® certified 100% post-consumer-waste recycled acid-free paper
Cover: FSC® certified 10% post-consumer-waste recycled paper

TABLE OF CONTENTS

Note: all poetry fragments are taken from
When You First Called Me Radha: Poems
by Swami Sivananda Radha

PREFACE

I CAN STILL REMEMBER how Swami Radha's face lit up when she talked about the Light. She seemed not so much to be relating her experiences as she spoke, but looking directly inward at a luminous place that I couldn't yet see. Later, she called it the Hidden Place, and wrote a poem about it that helped give me a glimpse of what she was talking about:[1]

> To find the entrance
> to that hidden place
> will demand mental acrobatics,
> taking risks, destroying concepts
> and unproven beliefs
> conquering fear of falling from
> the rainbow into abyss.

Remember
others before you
have done it, and did walk the rainbow,
their search sincere, their longing great
the loving desire gave them strength. ˙

Finally, lifetimes were
not wasted anymore.
The decision made
is crowned by a blessing.
The Pearl of Great Price is won.

This was in 1990 and '91, when I was definitely doing a
lot of mental acrobatics trying to reconcile what I knew as a
scientist with what I was starting to feel in my heart. Swami
Radha was patient with my struggles and compassionately
offered help in an unexpected way. She showed me a chapter ·
out of what seemed at first to be a dry academic book called
The Doctrine of Vibration, which discussed the ancient yoga and
philosophy known as Kaśmiri Śaivism.[2] With both a kind and
slightly mischievous look, she asked me to read it and tell her
what I thought about it.

It immediately struck me that what I was reading sounded
a lot like physics. Both systems appear to involve only one
energy, which can manifest in a wide variety of ways –
sometimes as particles, sometimes as forces, and sometimes as a
dazzling dance of transformation between them. Both hold that
the world is real, but that it is not what it seems and has many
levels of reality. And they both prominently feature vibrations
of many kinds and frequencies that serve to connect and bind
together all the different levels, forms and transformations.

Such vibrations can form waves and vortices and be coupled by resonances so that more elaborate structures can emerge from very simple underlying fields.

The only part that didn't immediately sound like physics to me was the assertion that this one energy was also the essence of consciousness, which the book called Śiva or the Divine Light. But if as a scientist, I hoped to understand what consciousness was, how could I fail to consider that it might be intimately linked to the same underlying energy as physics?

There ensued an ongoing dialogue over the next five years, during which Swami Radha gradually shared more and more of her insights and experiences about Light and vibration. Most helpful for me were the many poems that she wrote and recorded during this period. They gave me clues about the inner meanings of the esoteric Sanskrit words and helped me begin to unravel what the Kaśmiri texts were talking about and to relate it to my own personal experience.

I am delighted that Swami Lalitananda has now compiled Swami Radha's interwoven talks, thoughts and poems on Light and vibration into the form of a book. As Swami Radha herself often noted, words can at best be pointers to something we are just beginning to glimpse or aids in helping us remember things that at some level we already know. Swami Radha's words, in particular, are best read like poems – slowly and with a heart and mind receptive to flashes of intuition. I wish that you could hear her speaking these words, because so much can turn on a subtle pause or change of intonation. I especially encourage you to listen to the recording of her poetry that is now available.

But listening and reading are just a beginning. There is no substitute for practice in order to come to a deeper understanding. I'm still just beginning to discover how deeply the practices she described – such as following wonder back to its source – can lead, or how much spaciousness and compassion can arise when I let the Light fill my heart. Sometimes the light breaks through in ways that are unmistakeable, and sometimes things are cloudy and I feel like a scientist still looking into a brightly lit cathedral window from the outside. But I am absolutely convinced of the reality of the luminous world that she saw so clearly, and am very grateful that she tried so hard and in so many ways to help us to see it as well.

Swami Radha was never satisfied if we just took her word for things, and the teachings and practices related in this book are no exception. Like a scientist, and like she had done, she insisted that we do our own experiments and make our own discoveries. And having done so, that we integrate them into how we live our lives. In the end, this can become a lifelong project, and one of my first and most frequent discoveries is how much I still don't know.

Swami Radha in turn would sometimes insist that I knew more than I thought I did: it was just that I was having trouble *remembering*. I have found the teachings and practices described and pointed toward in this book to be excellent *memory* aids – and I hope that you will discover this for yourself, as well.

Prakasa (Tom Weaver)
February 15, 2007

---

1 "To Find the Entrance," *When You First Called Me Radha: Poems,* Swami Sivananda Radha (Kootenay Bay, BC: Timeless Books, 2005): 29.

2 *The Doctrine of Vibration,* Mark S.G. Dyczkowski (Albany, NY: SUNY Press, 1987).

INTRODUCTION

IN *LIGHT & VIBRATION*, Swami Sivananda Radha
contemplates the most subtle understanding of the universe,
and attempts to "explain the unexplainable," as she would
often say. Through metaphor and nuance, she offers a pathway
to Liberation, a way to connect the invisible and the visible.
Her own mystical experience of Light is the basis of the work,
which gives it an immediacy and authority that differ from a
mere theoretical or academic exercise. This book, like a poem
or sacred text, is full in its richness – a vessel brimming with
wisdom and saturated with questions that burst old boundaries
of thought.

Inherent in her vision is the elusive potential for peace.
If we can experience the world as Light and vibration, can we
then accept all paths and religions as unique expressions of that
oneness? If we first understand ourselves – our inner world

and the impact of our own thoughts and choices on the world – can we then create the kind of world we would like to live in: a world of peace and harmony, a world based on personal responsibility, understanding and compassion?

How does the mind interfere with this vision? And can that interference be turned around, so the mind's potential is realized? What could that potential be and how would we access it? Can simple tools such as practising mantra and studying dreams create clarity of perception? And when perception is clear, what would our experience be? Swami Radha encourages us to test our hypotheses like scientists. Do we have an idea of enlightenment? What will bring us closer to that idea? What if the ideas themselves are the obstacles?

I was with Swami Radha during her last years when the ideas in this book were fermenting and demanding form. I was excited by her daring spirit. She was willing to break conceptual boundaries and plunge into the unknown. On the one hand, she knew life so intimately and was surprised at nothing. On the other, she was intensely alive, involved and filled with wonder at everything life offered. Right up to her last breath, she remained eager to learn: How does physics view consciousness? What are the latest studies on the brain? How do different cultures construct systems of thought that both support and limit their worldviews? Where are the meeting places between religions?

In the late 1980s and early 1990s, many texts on Kaśmiri Śaivism were translated into English for the first time, and these texts resonated with her and became a springboard for her own reflections on Light and vibration, which had been the foundation of her life's work. The result was a series of recordings, often in dialogue with her physicist friend or students who were nearby. Sometimes alone in the night, she would capture fleeting ideas on her simple tape recorder, her voice resonating with the attempt to translate mystery into words. How is it possible to put the subtle into form?

LIGHT & VIBRATION is the culmination of Swami Radha's teachings on yoga and marks her preparation for her departure from the Earth – the transition from concrete to abstract, from form to formless – a transition which we all will inevitably face. When Swami Radha passed into Light in 1995, I knew that I needed to fulfill her wish to turn the transcripts into a manuscript so that other people could benefit. I struggled for years to put these various and subtle ideas into a structure that resembled a book. I needed time to grow and mature my own understanding. This past year, the material seemed to call and almost push me to start, to find a way. And so I began at the centre – at the impossible-to-describe source, the top of the mountain, Śiva/Śakti – because everything, it seemed to me, emanated from that centre.

In the Śakta teachings, I had always felt that the entire universe was explained, but I just could not understand it. But now, with Swami Radha's words acting as a key, I started to see more clearly how Energy could become more dense and take form, how Energy could sustain existence, and how it could withdraw to become one again. Endless waves of creation and dissolution. Her writing opened up what had seemed impenetrable and esoteric scriptures, and I could see how amazingly relevant these ancient teachings still are.

Swami Radha's vision is fresh and resonant with her own experience, but her knowledge is not new. This knowledge has always been there and only seems hidden because words cannot say it plainly, but rather must act as a mirror and catch the reflections of an elusive reality, a world more real than appearances.

Editing this book has been a blessing and an intense learning, for which I will always be grateful. My hope is that her words will help awaken the innate intelligence in every reader, and be a catalyst for our own exploration of the dance of Energy and form. How do the vibrations of oneness become the many and the many become one again, without ever having ceased to be itself?

Swami Lalitananda
February 4, 2007

PART ONE

THE ONE
& THE MANY

Which way to Truth?
Truth is One,
approaches are different.
Awareness is Divine Light shining.

1 ONE SOURCE

WHEN WE INVESTIGATE by looking closely at something, we break it into portions and then become busy with that limited section, forgetting that it is only part of the whole. The Western mind in particular specializes and habitually breaks things into sections and then forgets that the section is only a section, not the whole.

On a cosmic level, one source of Energy manifests the whole universe. This one source of Energy, without duality, radiates different manifestations. The one Energy vibrates and the different vibrations make it appear multiple and separate.

Again, we get caught in the differences and forget to look for the whole.

This book is a reminder of the oneness of the Light and an exploration of the vibrations that make the oneness appear so varied at every level. It is my hope that readers will be challenged to think deeply for themselves and to sharpen their perceptions in order to make their way back to the unity that is promised through Yoga.

Practice is more important than theory. Exercising the mind is like exercising a muscle until it can perform mental acrobatics. Any book can be an inspiration, but is only a starting point for your own thinking.

The essence of the original teachings can become watered down through time, in the same way that a message whispered from one person to the next ends up quite different by the time it reaches the last person. Study can stimulate thinking, but does not necessarily further your knowledge because it is not yet your own experience. You have to use your mind to make contact with your own inner source.

The original Light
reflections in different pulses.
The countless powers of the Divine.
The Divine Mind's pulsation
after a penetration to the core.
Narrowness, a point of Light.
First the Goddess innate
a sensation of expansion of mind,
then a Goddess of greater dimension.

2 ŚIVA & ŚAKTI

THE TWO ASPECTS OF CREATION – Energy and its manifestation – exist together. There is no manifestation, no creation, no world without the innate power. In a personal way, you have to think that without your essence, without spiritual Energy, you cannot function. Without Energy-as-such, you cannot form even one single thought. You cannot perform one single action. Without the brain telling the hand to move, the hand does not move.

Manifestation depends on Energy, but Energy also depends on manifestation; otherwise, we would not know the power is there. A house can be wired with all the electricity it needs and even more, but if there is nothing to which the power goes – no light, no heat, no appliance – would you know if there is any power? As human beings, we ourselves are of a double nature – Energy and manifestation.

We are responsible for how we allow our power to manifest. We cannot just run wild. The use of Energy is our choice and responsibility. People do not realize how great that responsibility is. When Energy goes into greedy emotions such as hatred, ambition and selfishness, these manifestations cover the Light. Energy is neutral and just as electricity can manifest as heat or cold, Energy can take opposite forms and yet is still the same basic Energy. How we use our personal Energy is our responsibility.

Our physical and mental houses have a lot of power, but if they are not connected to our ability to use that power, many aspects will not function. We cannot even know how much power we have in our mental worlds if we do not allow this power to manifest properly, which requires plenty of guidance in the beginning. We may eventually discover that there are many different powers connected to mind. Intelligence is just one power and itself manifests in varying degrees from a faint glimmer to the enormous power of the genius – yet it is still the same Energy.

We have to discover what this Energy is. Where do we take the Energy from to formulate thoughts? Is thought-energy exclusive or does it interact with the same Energy expressed in different ways? How much is thought stimulated by imagination and emotions, such as hope and fear? Energy can manifest along an incredible scale, like the scale of a grand piano. The total is always the same Energy, not split, but used differently and variable in strength.

The body is the vehicle for the brain. The brain is the vehicle for the perception and the manifestation of Divine Light, and that Light, to whatever small or great degree, is the link between human life and the cosmos.

When greed and self-importance are dissolved, self-awareness becomes evident. We have to see where self-importance, greed and false pride come from and how they interfere with our essential luminosity. Eventually we will discover that within every human being is a radiant deity, which just has to be permitted to shine by cutting off the heads of the ego and possessiveness. Then we can unearth the real nature of the power that is already ours. All that covers it has to be stripped away. Powers such as discrimination, compassion and understanding are realized continuously through self-reflection.

Ask yourself: Can there be knowledge without a knower? There is an interdependency between the two. That "something" in us, the knower, is also the indwelling essence in the mind.

ENERGY IS FORMLESS and form in its manifestation. But without manifestation, Energy would be unrecognizable. In the same way, we cannot describe pure space because we cannot perceive of pure space. We perceive of outer space because of the galaxies. But can we conceive of the end of space? Where would that end be? It is not recognizable through conscious awareness or perception.

In the Eastern teachings, the name "Śiva" is sometimes used to describe the reality of Energy as such. Śiva is never static. Energy is not static at any time, even in our own minds.

When we sleep, we dream. The vibrations of the mind will slow down, but the mind will not stop entirely. It just cannot. Life is a wave. The wave may become slower, longer, shallower, but the movement does not disappear.

If an approach to the universe as Consciousness is described through certain steps or states, what is being described or recognized is universal Consciousness from the vantage point of the lesser consciousness of the human being. The supreme Energy, Cosmic Consciousness, emanates in endless ways, but only a few of those emanations will ever be recognized by the lesser consciousness of even the most enlightened person.

If we call that accumulation of unlimited, immeasurable power Śiva, as viewed from the lesser vibration of a human mind, we tend to personify it so the human mind can communicate with it and about it. The moment we personify this immeasurable power, we reduce it to pieces – to a form that we can understand through our limited perception and our lesser consciousness.

When this Energy manifests through its different frequencies, the term "Śakti" (Power) is used. Unless creation is accepted and appreciated first, how can the Energy behind it be even faintly understood? The source of power is difficult to recognize; not so the manifestation of the power.

Śakti, the vibrational power of Consciousness, is often personified as a goddess. The Light of Consciousness is the creative power that is always spontaneous in its projection and manifestation. The vibrating power of Consciousness manifests when all other thoughts, patterns and attachments to ideas have faded. When Śakti arouses, we are truly spontaneous and that spontaneity vibrates to stir others. If I am terribly upset and my emotions are highly aroused, I can ignite your emotions. But in the same way, if I am inspired I can ignite something very positive in you. Both are possible. Śakti is creation, preservation and constant change. All manifestation is a constant flow.

Consciousness is always. Consciousness is Energy vibrating at different frequencies, existing also, and to be discovered in matter. Consciousness is self-luminous, but there are degrees of luminosity and a range of frequencies. Eventually we will merge with our luminous Consciousness.

Śakti's vibrations are the most vivid expression of the waves of life itself. In deep meditation we can get a glimpse of universal Consciousness, an inner blissful vibration. The vibration of Cosmic Energy is the source and power of everything manifest from the smallest particle to the entire universe.

We must be able to experience awe and wonder.

THE ONENESS OF ŚIVA AND ŚAKTI is described like fire and heat, which cannot be separated. From this perspective, Śiva and Śakti are not different, and are only the names of philosophical ideas. The male/female principles are not separate entities but are a unit – the same source of Energy manifesting different qualities. Power simply is. It is not male or female. Just as the air is not he or she and the air can have various conditions, so Energy and power are not separate.

Water can become ice, snow or steam, but we do not confuse the fact that it is basically water. Yet if I am looking out over a lake, can I see the two gases in water? There is no trace of either once they have united. This is like Śiva/Śakti in union and also relates to the union of the physical and the spiritual within ourselves. Without this human being that makes his or her own mistakes and takes a course of action seeking a purpose in life, the Light would not have a vehicle to express itself.

In Kuṇḍalinī Yoga symbolism, the union of Śiva and Śakti is represented as unity in one body – half man and half woman. The meaning of this symbolism is lost today. True oneness is only achieved in a particular state of mind for which the sexual act is not essential. Sexual pleasure, which is often misinterpreted as spiritual union, is in fact only the registration of stimulation in the pleasure centre of the brain. The experience of union has many levels, beginning with the union of the masculine and feminine united within oneself. The final experience is when the individual Consciousness unites with Cosmic Consciousness, which is beyond the limitations of language to describe.

INSTEAD OF "ŚIVA" we can also use "Light" as a symbol of Energy-as-such. Light is the most subtle symbol for Energy. But it is still not sufficient to explain the existence of the universe, which appears to be the vibration of that Energy which itself may be Light-producing.

How are Light and Consciousness related? The very nature of Consciousness is Light. It is not that Light is here and Consciousness is there and Light shines on Consciousness. Here is awareness and that awareness is Light. Light also vibrates outside ourselves. The cosmos vibrates, the earth vibrates, the moon vibrates. Light descends into matter, and because matter has a central Energy, matter can also ascend into Light. That flow of Energy, which we can call Cosmic Consciousness, is ever creating new forms and waves of actions, thoughts, vibrations, ideas.

By practising awareness, by allowing an interpenetration of vibrations and not putting ideas into pigeonholes, we can come closer to understanding Cosmic Energy. But we cannot ever discover all of Cosmic Energy – that is not possible for the mind functioning on a three-dimensional level. But without training and effort, the mind cannot enter a fourth or fifth or even sixth dimension.

WHEN YOU HAVE MONEY, you have to skillfully manipulate it to increase it. If you have some knowledge, you can increase that knowledge until it becomes an incredible resource.

First by increasing our awareness, we can discover within ourselves the Light of understanding. We can understand more profoundly what we thought we had already understood. Eventually as this profoundness of understanding increases, we will find we have gained knowledge. This is gaining knowledge through mental clarity. From that knowledge we can experience more and more deeply, so our understanding of our limited experience increases. The entire process is also partly an expression of will to attain the highest knowledge we possibly can. Some knowledge will come only from other sources and will entice us toward greater experience.

The Light projects onto the screen of human Consciousness. Yet reception can only take place by degrees, and those degrees have to be developed. Our own active participation in our evolution can help us achieve the goal and purpose of life. This enormous potential is within our reach.

How can we enter into the centre of this force, above all space, time, names and forms? We have to look first at where we are and what we can understand. Can we understand the vibration that moves the cosmos if we do not understand how this vibrational force manifests in ourselves – in our bodies, in our minds, in our senses, in our emotions? Slowly the picture has to come together.

Are You not painting
Your own picture in my mind?
Who else is it if not
the creative power of Your maya?

3 MĀYĀ

COSMIC CONSCIOUSNESS exists as pure Energy vibrating in space. Known as Śakti in its manifest diversity, this power becomes Māyā – usually interpreted as "illusion" – when we forget that the Light is present, only covered by the clouds of our emotions and ignorance. Māyā is like adding colour to water, creating the idea of duality.

Who has accepted the essence? Just as electricity can be falsely mistaken for its manifestations as light, heat and movement, we can see that it is only our mistaken concepts and perceptions that make Energy appear as limited form.

Māyā means seeing the form without the essence. We can be drawn into Māyā, like children distracted by toys. Our interest becomes diverted and we engage in play, forgetting our purpose. But we also have the potential to recognize and understand the absolute creative power behind Māyā, the self-renewing power of Consciousness. From this perspective, the world as creation has a reality but not an absolute Reality.

It is only by discrimination that the path beyond all illusions can be found. Time and space are very illusory. What we think takes place in an instant may not be instantaneous. What has gone on before from a present-day view of life is considered the past, while from the view of eternity perhaps there is no past.

We can look at Māyā as the deluding aspect of the creative power. Often symbolically presented as a projector of dazzling colours, the yogic masters warn us about getting involved in these colourful displays. What was a practical warning in ancient times is even more relevant for us today, with the stimulation available through advertising, entertainment and technology. We need emotional detachment to be free of Māyā's powerful influences.

Māyā reigns in the physical, the mental and the emotional worlds, and the texts tell us to conquer or dismantle these three worlds. To do so, we need to understand that whatever exists has its beginning in the unseen. Illusions and desires give creative Energy its shape and form, just as a pot is formed from clay. We can change the shape as long as the clay is soft and we work with it, but once a concept has been fired in the kiln of emotions it requires great efforts to destroy.

The physical, mental and emotional worlds are not really separate, but are interrelated aspects of the world of our own creation. The world we live in is our perception, and we project our own concepts onto it. We are responsible for what we project, even on a daily level to the people we interact with. We are responsible for the vibrations we emanate – our tone of voice, our facial expressions, our actions. Everything we do is an expression of ourselves – manipulated by egocentricity, by compassion, by understanding, by hatred, by whatever quality we choose. All the different qualities arise from the same Energy.

The illusions we indulge in are endless, and they play out on a very basic level. The most creative force we have is the force that can produce life through sexual activity. Everything in nature reproduces itself and procreation is necessary to keep life going. But can that force be lifted up from the very basic level? Is there more? Think of the illusions that are generated around sex. Men and women imagine the perfect dream lover and then are disappointed when their human partner cannot fulfill the image. People struggle to accept themselves and feed into suggestions that clothes or cosmetics or cars will make them more attractive.

The power of Māyā is enormous. Many people do not recognize their illusions for what they are because the desire for recognition, acceptance and value stands in the way. Some people dream of a paradise where everything is beautiful and perfect. Or worse, they imagine that if everyone else were like them, there would be no difficulties in the world.

Illusions like these keep us on a teeter-totter between what our imagination dictates and what we actually experience. When the teeter-totter goes down and the fantasies are dispelled, we are disappointed. When our illusions are shattered, our despair is usually the greatest. But when that despair ends, awareness can come in. It does not make sense to try to glue the shattered pieces of illusion back together. They will never be the same.

Another of the biggest illusions is that the intellect can understand everything. The intellect is a tool, but it has no Light of its own just as the moon has no light without the sun. The intellect can create enormous illusions, and even though the illusions do not affect the inner Light, the fantasies can turn into heavy burdens that make it more difficult to approach the Light uprightly and openly. We need to stop giving our intellectual powers too much importance and instead turn our gaze within. There may come a point when the intellect demands tangible evidence and denies all spiritual experiences. But how can the intellect explain the mystical, which, like a flower's fragrance, can emanate beyond form?

How can we understand the inherent power in our own illusions and take responsibility for them? It is the emotions in conjunction with the imagination and mental powers that bring illusion into existence. To conquer the emotional world, which is often quite murky, we have to bring in the Light – the light of understanding, the light of working with our own evolution. But then comes a temptation. From the glimmer of understanding we gain, we become victim to the illusion that we are already enlightened. It is not easy to meet ourselves at the gut level.

To accept the hard facts seems to be unnecessarily cruel. But it is the illusion itself that is the source of pain. Pain is caused by ignorance and by staying intentionally blind when experience has already taught us something different. For too long we have thought that we are victims of circumstance, when we actually have allowed ourselves to remain ignorant, seldom applying discrimination and conscious investigation to our experiences. We are too busy to go into depth, and instead try to escape pain and disappointment by hoping it will go away. If intelligence were used properly, there would be investigation, leading to a clearer perception of reality instead of a false one which causes more pain.

Usually we are seeing through a veil, as if through sheer curtains with more sheer curtains behind them until finally the picture becomes hardly visible anymore. It is not that some greater power gives us information or a message or warning or invites expectation, then puts a veil over it. It is just that our ordinary perception and judgement form the veil. We find it easier to see a person's shortcomings than to see their spiritual existence.

In the early years of spiritual life, the desire for reassurance is very strong. We may want confirmation that we have done the right thing, or that we are not deluded or overly imaginative. Then later, when the mind is further developed, we may establish a set of principles and ideas as guidelines for our understanding. These very principles become one of the veils that eventually has to be cut off.

We can be aware enough to know that we ourselves have put up the veils or screens. The desire to remove the screen will help it disappear. But the human mind will always be afflicted with occasional doubts and questions about our own worth. The more you become aware of the enormous power of Cosmic Energy the more you may wonder, "How can this human mind even approach it?"

DO ILLUSIONS HAVE ANY REALITY? What is the creative Energy of illusions? Māyā is a great power, yet it is the same power as the Light. Just as the sun has many rays, so does the power of Consciousness have many manifestations. What will not die is the power beyond Māyā. And Māyā, too, assumes a cosmic role – projecting another round of birth with death to follow. Will it be a life of darkness? Semi-darkness? Or a mixture of light and shadow until the Divine Light consumes all that obstructs it?

In every religion, the idea of being consumed by Divine Light is imagined as stories of heaven, whether it is the Christian heaven, the heaven of Allah, the heaven of Kṛṣṇa, Śiva or Rama. But what would a region of Light, and only Light, mean? Nothingness? Emptiness? Emptiness without projection? A formidable thought for the human mind that always seeks shelter and a place to construct its own weavings. But such abstract speculations are usually misleading. Only personal experience can convince. Even then, we cannot be sure that Māyā did not have a part in it. How can we know when our experiences are self-created?

Is life a dream of Māyā? Are dreams a reality? Where does reality begin and where does reality end? Searching for the answers to these questions can be fascinating, but the answer is of little consequence as the inspiration is in the process.

Can mind follow its own
creation? But to where?

4 IMAGES & LIGHT

MĀYĀ CAN DELUDE US into seeing only differences, but we can use our personal Māyā as a stepping-stone to create equally colourful images to represent the Cosmic Energy (the Divine in whatever name and form), for the focus of our own mind. By creating an image of the Divine, that which the image represents can actually manifest. If we think of the Divine in any form, it is like putting a face on a balloon. Inside is still the invisible power.

If the fabric of the mind is ready to allow a creative fantasy of the Divine in whatever shape and form, it is a first step to opening the door. As long as we realize that the image is created in our own mind, it is very useful.

By creating a symbol that is pleasing to the mind, we also help bridge the gap between our philosophical understanding and our emotional needs. We can create an image, for example, of Divine Mother giving birth to all life. Or we can create a temple and visualize Her sitting within, then filling the entire sky. The whole earth can become our temple. Or we can create more abstract symbols in the same way that scientists create symbols for electricity or for particles, which nobody has ever seen. Creating symbols to communicate with the Most High is a very natural response. And if our emotions become deeply involved and greatly satisfied, we cannot help but become connected to our creation. This is Māyā at Her most beautiful, Māyā at Her most supportive, inspirational and uplifting. She keeps us breathless in awe and wonder, in spite of our knowing that it is our own projection. But powerful illusions have the ability to manifest something real.

The mind has its own demands – it will accept only what is pleasant and enjoyable. We can admire a stone or piece of rock for its beauty, the veins, the different shades and colours, but it is more difficult to see the Energy that is innate in this rock. Once we have carved it into a human likeness, our whole attitude changes because the demands of sight and emotions are satisfied. We could take a piece of wood – an ordinary piece of wood that we would throw into the fireplace – and because of its innate Energy, we could use it as a symbol of Cosmic Energy. But it would not give us emotional satisfaction or satisfy our sense of sight. It would not entice us into worship or devotion. When we give wood the shape and form of a statue and give it a name according to our culture, it becomes more satisfying to the mind.

THE MIND ALWAYS NEEDS SOMETHING to focus on. That makes it extremely difficult to have a true understanding of Cosmic Consciousness. Cosmic Consciousness does not have an image. It is not something that we can look at, measure or touch. But if we cannot relate to the Divine in some way, our concepts will have no meaning in our lives. So we create images. If your mind becomes very critical and says, "You have created this image in your own mind and there is nothing to it," stop for a moment and think how the mind is constantly creating. Think about how much criticism the mind creates. At least when it is creating an image of the Divine Power, it has moved from being involved with illusions on a lower level to being involved with the desire for something more elevated.

Imagining the Divine in our mind depends on the mind's ability to intricately create, just as we would if we were creating a piece of art or jewellery. And as the mind becomes more mature, the image will develop, just as technology develops over time.

You can embellish and beautify your image until it becomes your very own. Your attachment to it can be very elevating and supportive of your spiritual life. When you need personal comfort, you can seek the comfort in this Divine aspect. Even if the mind keeps creating images that are more beautiful, more intricate, more powerful, let it happen. The mind makes progress by delighting in an image of the spiritual power that is pursued. It is much better for the mind to be busy with this activity than to be scheming for self-gratification and speculating about worldly achievements.

Even religions that forbid images cannot avoid them. A temple is an image, a book is an image, writing is an image, and the religious leader himself or herself is an image. The mind needs something to hold onto and to interpret in a way that is closest to its own level of understanding. People become confused and often superstitious until the mind is trained.

By using the imagination, we open the door for the Divine to reveal itself. The imagination is only useful as long as it helps us to open this door. Without preparing the mind, a sudden experience of the entire cosmos would cause us to collapse. Even people who experience psychic phenomena do so little by little, so the shock is taken away.

The problem comes only if we fool ourselves into thinking our image is truly God. The insistence that any single image is the only way to perceive the unlimited Cosmic Energy has to be renounced. Holding onto an idea of the Divine presence may prevent us from actually experiencing it. Insisting on a particular form is like commanding the Divine, which is impossible.

Any image of the Divine that we create is as impermanent as everything else in life. Nothing that is perceptible through the senses lasts forever. And as we grow and mature, our concept of the Divine will also grow and mature. We perceive the greater power differently at different times, influenced by our life experiences and our change in perspective. Therefore the image will also change. It has to. But there may also be moments when we have a sudden powerful knowing, when there is no image and yet we *do* know.

Light is the most subtle symbol of Energy-as-such. Starting with a concrete image helps the mind become more steadfast, more single-pointed, more focused. Once the mind has become focused and has absorbed more of that invisible power of Divine Energy, we can visualize the image in the Light. This will help to break any dependency and to leave the image behind. Light is the best symbol to assist in going beyond the concrete image.

Light is a subtle image, but it is an image that even the untrained mind can hold because as human beings we all are influenced by the light of the sun and moon. We live by symbol and metaphor to a much greater degree than we admit. If we take the sun as a symbol of the source of Divine Light and the mind as the moon that reflects that Light, we can learn to make our mind receptive and become a reflector of the Light of Divine Knowledge.

By visualizing the Divine image in the Light, we gradually move away from constantly satisfying the sense of sight and the emotions. When we concentrate on the image, we will see that it is made of a combination of energies. Eventually the form will dissolve into Light. We can let the Light oscillate so that sometimes we see the image, sometimes the Light. That oscillating vibration starts to tap into the capacity of the mind to move between the concrete and the abstract. When we can move between these two worlds, it is possible to find the centre and not be thrown off by either.

When we reflect on the Light within ourselves, we can start to go beyond old limitations. First it requires practice – training and preparing, as we do when learning to drive a car. We start by following instructions; later we can develop our own style. And as we focus on the Light in ourselves, we will eventually recognize that the Light is who we are.

Once we connect with this power in ourselves, then "Namaste – the Divine in me salutes the Divine in you" will become meaningful. If I want the Divine in me to recognize the Divine in you, I first need to make an effort to discover the Light in myself. And then I need to discover the Light, not just in those people who accept me, but also in those with whom I would rather not associate.

PRACTICES LIKE THE DIVINE LIGHT INVOCATION[1], a standing meditation where we visualize Light and affirm our connection to the Light, help us to understand that the Light is within ourselves. This same idea can be traced in many religions. Jesus said the kingdom of God is within. How do we find that kingdom of God within? On the Buddhist path, the image of the Buddha stands for a state beyond mind. What does a state beyond mind mean?

When we focus on Light, we become sensitive to the more subtle vibrations that are present. We have them but often we do not use them. If we are rattling with strong emotions or powerful attachments, we will not be able to contact the finer vibrations of the heart.

Can we conceive of a teaching of Light and vibration that includes the immense variations of life, and move away from the doctrines that separate us? Over the centuries, every religion has given different names to countless gods and goddesses, many who have since disappeared and been replaced by others. If, instead of the word "god" or "goddess," we use the word "power," then we are closer to understanding that the differences are only apparent. If every name and form of the Divine is the power of Light – if God is Light, the Buddha is Light, Jesus is Light, Śiva is Light, Saraswati is Light, Allah is Light – the Light from all religions can pool together. The Light can unite us.

_____

1   See Appendix: The Divine Light Invocation, page 163.

PART TWO

VIBRATIONS & LIGHT

Light pulses
sound vibrates
can you hear the sun sing?

5 VIBRATION & SOUND

COSMIC CONSCIOUSNESS and human consciousness are never in a state of permanence, but always in flux. As you sit reading, think that your body is impermanent and so is the functioning of your brain. But is there something more? Here is a very simple illustration to start your thinking. If you prick your finger, one drop of blood comes to the surface through the skin, but you know that is not all the blood you have. And there is still another part of the body that is constantly producing more blood.

Your mind vibrates and your emotions also vibrate,

wanting to jump in and either confirm or oppose a thought, and therefore stimulating the production of further thoughts. But you have to ask if there is anything more to you than that? What is the real you beyond the body, beyond the emotions, and beyond a certain level of the mind?

Find out where the Energy comes from that manifests as thoughts and emotions. Trace it back. How do you choose to use the Energy that comes to you without even having earned it? Do you use the Energy to nourish negativity? Even when you think you are giving the Energy to something positive, like love, is it really love? How do you differentiate between love and emotional attachment?

Is there a centre within yourself where the Energy is never diminished? If you observe your mind, you can see that even when one part of the mind is asleep another part is active. Something else from another region vibrates, even if we cannot always determine where it comes from.

BY PATIENTLY UNDERSTANDING your inner being and your outer existence, you can start to observe the interplay of forces between the inner and outer and see how that affects you. As human beings, we are part of this earth. We are part of the animal kingdom. We are part of the seasons. Our physical bodies are connected to the cycles of nature, so we need to accept the reality of the laws of nature. By observing ourselves, we can find out how our own cycles work. Do mood swings, for example, relate to the time of day or to the season?

The energy fields that surround our beautiful earth include electrical fields, magnetic fields, the Van Allen belts. There are radio waves of many different kinds and frequencies. There is gravitational force. All of these vibrations and their different frequencies influence us.

On some days you probably notice that everything flows easily, while on other days the same work becomes very heavy. Could it be because there are vibrations unknown to us that influence our physical body, our mental body, our emotional body? Even changes in atmospheric pressure can have an influence that we are subjected to. There is also an interplay of forces among people and a demand for constant response, which is not necessarily beneficial. It is like being in an argument that never ends – there is always something more to say. Information overload can lead us to a point where we are unable to respond at all anymore. We have no energy left. We need rest.

Ordinarily our five senses are constantly bombarded. We live in a noisy world and each noise has its own rate of vibration. Our houses vibrate with sounds from computers, heaters, fans, refrigerators. We are fighting a battle that has already dulled the senses, perhaps to the point where we think, "I don't hear it; that kind of noise doesn't disturb me." No, not anymore. But dulling the senses also means that you are dulling yourself to many higher perceptions.

While I was in India an old yogi offered me the opportunity to meditate in his cave. Later he asked me how it was. I answered rather wistfully that it was enchanting, particularly because of the sweet song of the birds. He pointed out that the cave has a long, very narrow entrance and birds would not fly into the darkness. The rocks were so polished that no bats lived in this cave. "Are you sure you heard something?" "Oh yes." I could almost imitate the sound, like young birds chirping in the early morning. He smiled and said,

"Did it never occur to you that rocks can sing?"

In the state of intense concentration, our senses can reach a height of sensitivity that we would normally fiercely dispute. Only testing will give you the proof. You may not necessarily travel to India, sit in a cave and hear the rocks sing, because you may have a different temperament. Your own laboratory apparatus may be quite different. But exploring the vibration of forces in your own nature is a good starting place.

Our own creative forces are enormous, yet we usually have little awareness of them. In our personal development we experience different rhythms – times when we move, times when we stand still, times when we go back, and times when we advance again. Consciousness also has its own frequencies and it is interfered with by other influences – by the vibrations of other minds, by the vibration of our own emotional responses, by the vibration of sound.

WE ALSO LIVE in an interior world of thoughts, imagination and illusions that have their own reality. The mind is invisible, yet all of our mental and emotional reactions vibrate in our being. Each of us is a vibrational powerhouse fueled through our mind, emotions and five senses. By becoming more aware at all times of what is vibrating in us, we can create a solid foundation that will eventually lift us beyond our ordinary way of thinking.

You can begin by investigating vibrations that are very personal, for example, your heartbeat. Check your pulse in the morning before getting up, then again after each meal. The early morning pulse gives the natural rhythm of your system. To discover which foods your body has difficulty handling, observe if your heart rate increases after eating. What else makes your pulse speed up? Sometimes we may appear calm, but the heart can be racing.

Do bones vibrate? When you chant mantra, try putting your fingertips lightly on your face and then on your skull. Resonance is easily felt in the skull. If you increase your sensitivity to touch, you may feel the vibrations in your shoulders or elbows, knees and hips. In fact, if you understand the principle, you can direct the vibration of the mantra into the parts of the body that need it most. Become aware of how the body responds, how the many cells in the body vibrate. Even when the sound becomes very faint, feel the alertness, the listening and the awareness growing.

Can you also become aware of how you project energy outwardly to others? Perhaps it is through a smile that demands attention, as if to say, "Look at how nice I am. Don't you feel you should talk to me or say hello or smile back?" In the Kuṇḍalinī Yoga system, one of the powers of the cakras is invisibility. To become invisible means to refrain from being heard, from being seen, from being noticed and appreciated – not to feel overlooked by others, but to intentionally contain yourself so you are not always giving out vibrations that demand a response.

The rhythm of the breath is also important to observe. Emotions make the breath vibrate in certain ways. You can calm the restlessness of the mind by consciously calming the breath. What is breath? Breath has power and is enormously vital. Without breath, you can achieve nothing. What vibrates in the breath when it flows into your body? What are the vibrations in the outflowing breath? Can you make a conscious attempt to inhale goodness, to exhale selfishness, to inhale inspiration, to exhale despair? Can you link the ingoing and the outgoing breath with the opposites of your emotions? Can you discriminate between what benefits and sustains you and what hinders and destroys you?

Between the ingoing and outgoing breath, there is a centre of stillness. That stillness, when the breath is held, allows for unexpected perception. "Between two breaths, realize." This is the potential of the space between breaths.

THE RHYTHM OF THE BREATH makes different sounds. Sound is vibration and vibrations are the Energy of the universe. When we are born and breathe, we make a sound. The baby's cry is our first language. Then we learn to use breath and sound to achieve comfort – crying when we are hungry or uncomfortable and making little "Aaah" sounds when we are happy. As the baby grows and identifies things, language begins to develop.

When we speak, we create sound by a collision in the throat. Air hits the obstacle of the vocal cords, which vibrate. We learn to manipulate the air and obstacles so cleverly that we can put sounds together and convey a message, a word, a desire. We can even modulate the sounds and "sing" music.

Sound and emotions blend together to make up the human voice, the instrument we use to express ourselves. The human voice is dependent on breath, which connects us with time. It takes time to fully inhale and exhale and to produce sound.

Become aware of your own voice. Different emotions vibrate in the sound of the voice, which is powered by the breath. When we are angry, we fire off our words in rapid succession. When we want something, we soften the voice, searching for the right words and the right tone – *would you please?* – implying that because we have asked so sweetly, how can anyone say no? We can be quite manipulative and dishonest in our presentation. When we want something, we try to extract it. We exercise control.

Unfortunately, most people do not want to control their own mind and emotions, which is where control is really needed. When you become more aware of your speech and recognize what it indicates about your state of mind, you gain awareness in increments. If you develop your sense of hearing by paying attention to it, you will know when your voice is expressing agitation, even if the person you are addressing does not pick it up. Then you have choice – do you want to continue to emanate this vibration?

Choose any mantra or prayer. Speak it or chant it for an hour or more. Record yourself and afterward listen to your voice. What do you hear? Your voice can express anguish, longing for the Divine, doubts ("Is there really something to this? Am I living a fantasy?") Find out which of your emotions resonate back to you. Listening to your own voice can tell you the range of your emotions, the type of your emotions, the strength, the softness, or gentleness of your emotions. You can learn to distinguish between them in the same way that a musician can tell an "E" from a "B." Your voice can become so refined and melodious that you will be able to express yourself through it very beautifully.

In human relationships listening is extremely important. Many complications and misunderstandings come in life by not listening. Listening intuitively is not everybody's strength, but it can be developed. Can you listen? Can you really hear? Can you tune in and be sensitive to the vibrations in another person? Whatever the mind perceives is also interpreted by describing it inwardly to ourselves. With hearing, we often hear only what we want to hear. Can you train yourself to hear even the most unpleasant sound or words?

The vibration of another person's voice tells you what they think about you. Someone can say your name very softly, kindly or casually. They can say it begging, pleading, demanding, angry, or expressing all their potential aggression into the sound. And yet only one word has been pronounced. The vibration in the voice tells you whether you are accepted or rejected, whether you need to pay attention or protect yourself. When you are called by your name and the sound is warm and loving, you may feel touched, reverberating with the sound. The mind is attracted and readily united with the caller.

Observe the vibrations that emanate from the way you think. It is essential to understand the vibration of your thoughts. Without that awareness, discrimination is not possible. If you imagine sounds in your mind, you may believe they are not heard. But are they heard with the inner ear or with the hearing centre in the brain? When you think, can you hear yourself think? Do you pronounce the words in your mind? Do those waves make sound? Is the uninterrupted stream of consciousness sound? When the mind is still, is there any sound? Is there a "pure" sound? Would it relate to harmony, or is harmony just order and key?

The power of speech is in the mind and does not need a tongue. The power of hearing is in the mind and does not need an ear. When you understand this, a new world opens up.

In Kuṇḍalinī Yoga, the Heart Cakra is called Anahātā, which means "unstruck sound," a sound produced without striking two objects together. What could this sound be? Is there a self-originating sound and where would we look for it? From my experience of hearing the rocks sing in the cave in

India, I began to understand that everything has its own sound. In the Kuṇḍalinī system these are called "seed sounds."

Whatever moves creates sound, but only certain vibrations are perceptible to the human ear. We know that many animals have a wider range of hearing than we do. As human beings we are deaf to many subtle sounds, especially if our self-centredness is great.

Our life experiences also create vibrations that continue to resonate in us. Those who had an alcoholic or very violent parent, particularly in their early years, may find the resonance from these experiences devastating. Through therapy it is possible to free oneself. But we cannot clear away the resonance of the past by force or by will. The vibrations encompass us in a way that we cannot easily step out of. The solution is to open ourselves to a very different kind of resonance, such as the vibrations of mantra or prayer.

As you start to understand sound and consciousness, you can learn to dialogue with the Light or Divine being in yourself. It is like learning a new language, a new way of communication. Just as sound is audible, but you cannot touch it, so is the development of Consciousness subtle but real.

Vibrations surround us continuously. By becoming aware of your own vibrations, you can exercise some control. If you emanate the best of yourself outward to others, you open yourself to receive the same back. Surrounding yourself in a screen of Light will allow only the best to pass out from you and in toward you. Then, if you do react in an uncontrolled way, you can take responsibility for ignoring the Light. If you visualize each person you talk to in a spiral of Light and let the spiral enlarge to include yourself, you will find that eventually even your worst enemy will change.

In my heart is a song
that speaks of my dream
to be forever with You.

6 MANTRA

SOUND AND LIGHT ARE VIBRATIONS, and vibrations
are different frequencies of Energy. Just as there is always
some electricity in the air but it will only manifest as thunder
and lightning under certain conditions, this also applies to
Kuṇḍalinī, the latent Energy within ourselves. Kuṇḍalinī
is both Light and sound, and mantra, the divinely inspired
perfect word-sound form, is used to attain Her. Mantra is Śakti
power manifesting as sound. Mantras are Kuṇḍalinī herself, for
She is all language.

Ancient texts state that the universe came into existence

through the power of sound. Even a single sound has enormous power. Think of the range between the sound of thunder and the sound of silence. The most profound expression of that Energy is the cosmic Om, which is the origin of all other sounds and symbolizes the essential spiritual reality. The mantra Om is said to give birth to rays of Light, bringing illumination to the mind.

There are two aspects to every sound – the audible expression, and the subtle sound-essence (*śabda*) that carries the meaning and arises from the source or eternal spirit. When the spoken word is sounded within and without, contact is made with this power. The chanting and recitation of mantras activates and accelerates the creative spiritual force, promoting harmony in all parts of our being. With practice we are gradually converted into a living centre of spiritual vibration that is attuned to other centres of vibration vastly more powerful.

Mantras are sacred sound syllables in which great wisdom is locked up, wisdom that will reveal itself only if we understand exactly what we are doing. Mantra affects certain areas of the mind, refines the emotions and prepares us to become ever more receptive to Divine influences. If you concentrate on a mantra and recite it with real feeling and a clear mind, it is very difficult not to get involved in the process.

It is usually suggested to recite a mantra a thousand times a day for forty days, to gain results. By this effort we put ourselves on track. It is like an airplane, revving up, taxiing, preparing for take-off. Eventually our efforts will take off until we reach a point of effortlessness. When we reach that point, we have pierced through the barriers – the cultural, social and survival barriers that have been put up around the mind, and we will find the place where Light is always reflected.

Mantra is the most profound speech, sound at its highest, because it takes us away from the ego's selfishness and self-importance. It lifts us beyond all other existence. When that supreme sound really becomes sovereign, it can move the world, change lives, actions and thinking. It can turn us into completely new beings. It is like being clothed in a new cloth of thought and sound. We hear ourselves speak, but no longer the speech of self-importance in which the mind continuously engages, but the sound of our innermost being.

The mantra has several powers – the power we give it, which reflects back to us; the power of whoever perceived it initially; the power from the millions of people who have practised it since; and also the power from those who have attained liberation through the mantra. As a comparison, you can think that if 500 million people believe in Jesus, Jesus is a power even if he never lived as a human being. The teachings have become personalized through that symbol.

The power of the mantra will become apparent only if practised while keeping all other intrusions out. It is not the practice alone that brings benefit, but maintaining awareness and focus and staying with the words that we are chanting. If you chant OM, make space for OM alone, without other thoughts. Ask what it means that OM is the cosmic sound. Go into depth as you practise, using your intelligence.

Observe the effects of your practice in your daily life. This is the foundation. Doing a long practice by will alone will not bring many benefits. When mantra is practised with the right attitude, sincerity and persistence over time, the results will become a source of strength, joy and happiness. A desire to go further will develop naturally without the force of willpower.

THE POWER OF THE MANTRA sets awareness in motion. Not by automatic, emotionally uninvolved repetition, but by inquiring what the mantra really is. What am I reciting? What happens to the mind when reciting the mantra? When the outside world disappears, the inner world opens up – your own inner world. Then you can destroy the three worlds that you have been so involved in without any true benefit to yourself or others. These three worlds are the emotional world, the mental world and the world of self-created illusions.

The sound of each word has its own vibration, and that, too, has to be clarified. The vibrations are intensely coloured by our emotions. Can we trust emotions? Not really. We all know people who love us today and hate us tomorrow. When emotions are refined, they move into the heart, and the feelings of the heart differ greatly from the emotions. Emotions demand a response from others because there is a feeling that "by myself I don't know." When we enter the heart, we do know and need no feedback. It is as if the sun of awareness shines on the lake of emotions, and the water evaporating into air loses its heaviness and power to destroy. When we repeat a mantra, we have to know what the vibrations of our speech generate. Is it all emotions? Is it less emotion? Is there a hint of love? Is there an abundance of love? Is there an intense commitment to love? An intense commitment to achieving what we ask in the mantra?

Mantra chanting is a way to transform powerful emotions into finer feelings to fill the heart. The vibrations of the heart change the rate of vibration of your entire being. With recitation of mantra comes the feeling and the desire to create for this incredible power a place to reside. The Heart Lotus becomes the natural place. The heart, when filled with transcendent feelings, is the best place to experience the pulsation and vibration of the Light.

In mantra practice, the Light takes shape and form and vibrates in the human voice. That is why mantra must be spoken. Our sense of hearing must be influenced. Our sense of hearing must get the message clearly. Much later, when the first experiences have taken place, the words of the mantra can be thought in the mind, inaudibly. This silent language, the conversation we start with the Divine, will be very helpful.

Think about it again. The power of the mantra sets awareness in motion. Think of the vibration that your words create outside your human body. The sound that has been released with the breath: Does it fade, die out or continue the journey? When you chant the mantra, where will the vibrations of the mantra go? Will they reach the walls? Will they penetrate the walls or bounce off? Will the vibrations die? What space and time will it take for the mantra to emanate into the distance?

When I practised mantra for five hours a day, I became keenly aware that sounds have images. I have seen the sounds of Hari Om like soap bubbles, each one having only one colour and that colour vibrating very strongly. Some were tiny bubbles and some were very big. It started me asking: Once a sound is released, where does it go? What would happen if I could travel on one of those bubbles?

The luminosity experienced in mantra practice arises from sounds of a high frequency that affect the brain but are seldom remembered in waking consciousness. It often takes a long time before the mind lets us into that hidden place, to which waking consciousness has no access.

Mantra practice is like shooting at a target. To aim at a

target requires concentration, motionlessness. Both body and mind need to be under control. You can lose the sensations of the body and dim the report of the sense perceptions, but never lose consciousness. Stay aware.

The training of spiritual practice, after the first wave of enthusiasm is over, often leaves people feeling bored. If they chant a mantra, it becomes a dry, meaningless repetition. However, I found that when the mechanicalness is overcome, the body and a certain portion of the mind settle down. The body comes more under control, which later proves very helpful in meditation. By *meditation,* I mean not simply sitting and closing the eyes and seeing what happens. It is very difficult to put into words, because the words imply a greater activity inwardly than there actually is. Meditation is a condition that makes us conducive to coming into a greater expectation. A conviction develops that something is going to take place, so one sits in this expectation now that the body has become more responsive to it.

The mantra will eventually become creative in us, revealing itself through the practice. But it takes time to reach that point and it takes discipline to control the aspect of mind that likes to engage and interfere. This part of the mind may have a certain impression of what is going on, but it does not have the understanding. It is important not to demand answers, while it is all right to pose questions. The experience of the mantra revealing itself will answer in a way that is far more precise and detailed than can be expressed in words.

The exploration of sound and consciousness can lead to a whole different understanding of the world we live in and the world we create. At some point we may recognize that each human being is in essence a mantra, a very unique yet cosmic mantra. When we have this perception about ourselves, we cannot help but let go of old patterns and obstacles and enjoy the wonder of being part of the cosmic symphony.

The body disintegrates.
The Light of Consciousness will not.

7 THE MANTRA OF LIGHT

THROUGH PRACTICE, we are bound to have the effect that any mantra promises. The Divine Light Mantra promises a gradual recognition of ourselves as beings of Light. At first we may feel there is a gap between the human and the Divine being in ourselves, but if we can at least recognize the Light within, the next steps are possible. The most beneficial direction for using this neutral, formless Energy of Light is in the power of awareness.

Here are the words of the mantra:

I am created by Divine Light.
I am sustained by Divine Light.
I am protected by Divine Light.
I am surrounded by Divine Light.
I am ever growing into Divine Light.

By reflecting on each line of the Light mantra, we can eventually understand the words so completely that they become filled with the very substance of Light. The deep meanings, the subtle meanings, have to be grasped. If the knowledge is not there, we can go in search of it. From the very concrete, we will make our way to the very subtle. We open a part of the mind that we never realized was there. But it is. It is a hidden place in our mind waiting to be discovered.

As you recite the first line of the Divine Light Mantra – "I am created by Divine Light" – ask yourself questions. How does Divine Light relate to the idea of the soul? Has the soul any particular seat in the body? Can the soul err? Is there something Divine in me that will not err? Is truth approached by just accepting? Or do I find truth in proportion to the intensity of my search and investigation into what I say? I am speaking words that have been given to me, but what do they mean to me?

Translate this line – "I am created by Divine Light" – into words that make sense to you. Even if you have only a faint understanding of the meaning, if something inwardly responds, let it grow. It is like a tiny spark that will eventually become at first a little flame and then a roaring fire. We have to be passionate about our spiritual being.

If you are a concrete thinker, you may have a different approach from an abstract thinker. Discover your own unique way. You may imagine that you are a being of Light who is like a meditating yogi creating your earthly being. "You" are the result of the meditation of the spiritual being in you. Use your own imagery to make this idea real.

When you start to expand the Light of awareness, sometimes it can be a painful experience. It is as if you owned a house with many rooms, only to discover these rooms are filled with unwelcome guests, living in clutter and dirt and darkness. When you demand ownership of your house, they will fight. This is the battle. The Divine Light Mantra brings the Light of awareness into the darkness so you can begin to see what is there.

"I am sustained by Divine Light." The Light sustains us, but if the Light is not fed or connected, it will go out. The fuel is your enthusiasm, your desire for the Light, your effort and determination and persistence, your commitment to keeping the Light going. The Light is like a fire that needs attention. Sometimes you may come in at just the last minute when there is only enough ember to burn a few small sticks. You cannot put a big log on and hope for success. Once the flame becomes a little more active again, you can gradually add more.

We have to give ourselves the kind of spiritual food we need. Eventually we want to go beyond the sense perceptions and find the Light behind everything. Then every action becomes symbolic and the mind is constantly involved with the Divine.

Sometimes life is painful because the idea is reinforced on all sides that we are part of the earth, part of the sex-birth-death chain. It requires effort to remember that we are also beings of

Light and to recognize that Light, and nourish that which we recognize.

"I am protected by Divine Light." If this thought comes quickly in any threatening situation, it means you have done enough spiritual practice that it has become second nature. You will be able to think Light and change your response. The main problem is to remember to think Light. Forgetfulness can be a blessing in one way – if we can forget that we felt hurt by someone. But if we forget that which protects us, it is not a blessing. Everything has two sides. The mind has that polarity.

"I am surrounded by Divine Light." You may forget for a moment about the Light, but you can remind yourself again. Make a habit of putting the person you are talking to in the Light. It will definitely change your attitude. See everyone surrounded by Light.

"I am ever growing into Divine Light." Really think about it. Once you make that decision, it is a promise to the Divine that you cannot change. You must build it in your mind over a long period of time. When your life goes differently from what you had planned, it often means that the Light has taken over. So before continuing to say these words, be clear. Do you really want to grow into Light?

The purpose of life can only be participation in our own evolution, which we can do consciously. When we do this consciously we experience much less pain. Of course it takes time. When you make the decision, everything does not just drop away. Any teacher can only point the way and offer a map of how to get there. But the map itself is not the way, which is often forgotten.

LIKE ALL MANTRAS, the mantra of the Light will become a self-generating power. Many things will begin to change in your life. The contact with Divine Light, your Divine essence, will increase until your own words become rays of Light, words of wisdom, and you will become attracted to previously undiscovered places of Light from which that wisdom radiates. As you practise the Light mantra, it may entice you to think more about the Light, seeing how Light plays a large part in daily life and communication.

If doubts creep into your heart and mind, the Light will remove them. The ego that wants to hold dominion over everything it has controlled for so long can only be removed by the tremendous power and influence of the Light. Doubts and misunderstandings can arise from karma from various past lives. There may be regrets about past actions. Asking for forgiveness, even for wrongs that you cannot remember, will help dissolve this type of karma in the Light.

When you have practised the mantra of the Light and gone as deeply as you can in understanding what the mantra means, practise the mantra while you are falling asleep. Your dreams will come from an intuitive depth that gives more than psychological insights. When you wake up with the mantra in your mind, you can be reasonably sure that you have been holding the Light through sleep. It takes concentration, determination and power to be able to do that. And only somebody who is really dedicated to the Light will even try.

Gurus and images of the Divine can be seen in the Light so their physical appearance fades into Light. When you think of great teachers of the past, think that their bodies were an illusory concept, that they were actually a mass of Light. The expectation that one day you will experience your own body as a mass of Light can be kept in the back of your mind. Think of your physical body as a product of your imagination, and note any insights that help you feel your body is filled with Light. And if you eventually experience your own body completely filled with Divine Light, the event is so unforgettable, so overpowering, you will have no doubt that the experience came from something beyond the imagination. Then you will realize that the physical body is more of an illusion than the body composed of Light.

Truth is Light.
Light is the highest reality.
That Light makes all things
new and fresh. Fleeting moments.
Nothing is permanent.

8 LIGHT

WHAT IS LIGHT? Light is reflective awareness and wisdom radiates through the Light like a pulse. Wisdom is the source.

We can speak of the vision of Light, the inner Light, the Light of understanding, the Light manifest and unmanifest. We can ask if the Light reflects and what it reflects upon and question: Is the Light the ultimate source of all that is manifest? In the end, perhaps we can say it is, but it is not a statement that should be made too early. We cannot know the top of the mountain if we are only halfway up. The human tendency to understand before we experience is a trap because we make assumptions without true understanding. Knowing from experience is quite different.

Truth is approached by degrees. No one has all the truth all at once or all the time. Truth does not just descend on us. Light does not just descend on us. The Light of knowledge does not just descend on us. We have to want this Light so badly, so intensely, so much with our entire being, that we become a magnet and draw this Light to ourselves.

If we create a little Light in the centre of our hearts and we kindle this Light and put in every effort to increase the power, the brightness and the warmth of this Light, then we will attract a greater Light – the Light of Divine Wisdom. There are many sources of Divine Wisdom that we have not yet discovered. We have Light hidden in us, and we have to remove all the covers that have not permitted the Light to truly shine. There are many ways. One way is through self-development and self-inquiry. Who am I? What kind of person do I want to be? If I decide that I want to be a powerful magnet to attract Divine Light, Divine Wisdom, then I have begun with an idea that will lead to the experience.

Light is independent. The Light of understanding is the degree of openness with which the Divine is approached. Growing in understanding, becoming more enlightened, more aware, will lead us to the source from which all power emanates.

But the influences that we allow in can literally block out the Light until all that may remain is a very tiny seed of Light, so small that we may consider it insignificant. I once suddenly experienced a reflection of myself, not by standing in front of a mirror, but by seeing my body as if it were made of glass, transparent, with the energies moving visibly within. Then

I saw my brain, not as it is shown in anatomical books, but as a mass of concentrated Light. Little dots came in from the outside, hitting the brain, and each time turning that bright, beautifully illumined area into a dark one, as if somebody had sprayed ink or opaque colour there. And as I watched, I saw how little was left of the original beautiful mass of Light. The more dark sparks, the less Light.

How can we understand those influences from the outside? They are preconceived ideas, ego-loaded thoughts, emotionally loaded desires.

Something needs to be done to hinder those influences that poison the mind through uncultivated emotions, and through closing to the greater Light that is available.

The power of mantra will help do just that. To concentrate really means to focus on one thing – on Light or on one word and its powerful meaning – to keep out the influences that are not beneficial, that interfere with the Light, that weaken the Light, and finally dim it to a point from which it is very difficult to retrieve. But if you kindle a desire and love for the Light, for the truth, for knowledge, then the power of the mantra will give the awareness of how you can make your way back, and bring the Light of awareness into the mind, and let it grow. Let the flame be kindled by this Divine desire and by constant effort to keep the intruders out.

Everything that hinders us, including the influences of the senses, when kept under control by awareness, can also become tools to help.

The interplay of forces of the senses has to be understood. All the senses play a part in what we do, what we think, and the influences that come from the outside world. The senses are very greedy, and this greed is intensified by the emotional quality infused in them. But the vibrating power of Consciousness can only manifest when all thought patterns and attachments to ideas have faded.

Tremendous effort is required to have the experience of interacting with our inner source. It is only in that interaction that we are nourished, encouraged and revitalized. We are responsible for the intensity of our desire for the Divine, our intensity of our desire for knowledge, even if in the beginning curiosity was the motivation.

When we begin to practise and open to the Light, many incredible thoughts that we have never had before will come to us. And we will wonder: How can I know this? Where did this knowledge come from? Why did I have to wait so long? Because we have not laid the foundation, which is building character, becoming dependable, changing emotions into true feelings. Only then can we be compassionate. And when we have become compassionate, when we can love without expecting anything in return, we have become truly human.

During the many years in our lives when we have little awareness, when we just act and think mechanically, the human mind will not expand. When we start on our path – the road to the Light, the Royal Highway of Light – the mind quickly revolts. It becomes tired of not being able to do what it wants to do, and it makes tremendous efforts to shrink back again to its comfortable place – the status quo. The mind feels it will be destroyed. Think again. What is destroyed? Moving from darkness to Light is a change. The darkness is there, as long as we are in a human body. The power is one. Darkness has its own power, but if we give all power to the Light, then we create a change from which we will benefit enormously, including the senses, emotions and mental powers. Suddenly we can concentrate. Suddenly we can be focused. We no longer need an image. Light has penetrated the image, even if occasionally it oscillates a little. But even that will change into Light.

Light has great power. If we reflect, we tap into this power of Light, and we can see that life – all life – is movement and Energy. Life is a wave, not a straight line.

At some time we will discover our birth into the Light. We will recognize that the Light is there. But still we know that we have not yet reached our destination fully. We are still on our way. And when the body disintegrates, what will happen to this Light of Consciousness? Will it be with me? What does "me" mean? Am I the body? Consciousness is a different kind of "me." And that Light of Consciousness will not disintegrate. It will remain a vortex of Energy, a vibrating power that will propel me into different circumstances.

On a practical level, to live in the Light means to have nothing to hide. You do not need to be nervous about being found out, which is essential for inner peace, harmony and well-being. But if you do have something to hide, visualize it in the Light. The source of wrong action is being in darkness. Sometimes we have to go through darkness to appreciate the Light.

The experience of one's body as a mass of Light is not an end, but rather a confirmation that you are going in the right direction. If you are prepared to give yourself to the Light and do so truly from the Light of your heart, you are yielding to a power that is beyond anything you can imagine.

PART THREE

HEART
& MIND

Where is my heart?
Oh, not the one that beats
when excitement arouses it.
The real heart
that reflects knowledge of
true love without any 'because'
attached to it.

My real heart is
in the hidden place on the moon
where the moon truly reflects
the brilliant Light,
the Divine Source.

9 HEART

THE HEART symbolizes an ocean of Light and Consciousness. The heart is symbolic for the centre of the spiritual being – limitless compassion and knowledge beyond intellect. The heart inspires and is the symbol for love, the unconditional love that is only possible through the Divine Source.

There is a difference between the knowing of the intellect and the knowing of the heart. Mental acrobatics can make the mind more flexible and prepare it to leap out of its confinement of established perceptions and meanings, which are really only opinions. The heart does not need to participate in acrobatics. The heart is limitless. Compassion is limitless, even within our human confinement. But sometimes we can understand that unlimited power only if we personify it, which means limiting the Energy that we do not understand by putting it into a shape and form and giving it a name. Then the path of the heart becomes more understandable to the mind and more accessible to us as individuals. We obtain a sense of closeness.

By personalizing the Divine, we may understand the compassion in reincarnation. Like a good father or mother, the Divine will say to its child, "This is wrong. You must not do it again. I will give you another chance." To be given another chance is probably the highest expression of compassion. We may be given chance after chance, many, many times. How many lifetimes? That depends on our response to Divine Compassion and our willingness to increase awareness, to increase the Light of understanding, and to thereby create a source of Light within ourselves, making that source a magnet to attract more Light. For me, the evidence of Divine Love is being given this chance to improve and to correct mistakes, especially if we have gone against the Divine Law. We may not even understand all of our mistakes in one lifetime.

In Kuṇḍalinī symbolism there is a small lotus called the *kalpataru*, or the Wishing Tree underneath the Heart Lotus. It is symbolic of the process of discovering the Divine within, and the mysteries and the awesome powers of the mind. Perhaps it is only when we reach a certain stage of development that we *wish* to know the greater wisdom. That desire to know, like any other desire, is a persistent force – we must persist until we attain the fulfillment of this desire. But this type of desire does not fulfill itself quickly. We have to be very earnest. It is like climbing a mountain. When we start off, we camp more often. When we are closer to the summit and have freed ourselves from the extra baggage – untested beliefs and opinions – we travel much lighter. The final ascent, though, may be straight up on sheer rock or ice, with nothing to hold onto. But the vibrational power that is accumulated in the heart will serve us well enough to complete the journey.

To understand the vibrational power accumulated in the heart, compare it to emotional power. Emotional power arms us with weapons to attain the goal of emotional satisfaction, whether that is finding a partner, robbing a bank, or becoming the president of a country. If emotions can generate this much power, we cannot underestimate the power of the heart.

If we look at the heart as symbolic of the essence of the vibrating cosmic rhythm – because the heart has its own rhythm – we can see that many different manifestations emanate from the heart. There are sources from which knowledge radiates to us. Some of these sources are not to be sought outside ourselves, but rather are to be discovered in our own heart.

To understand the Divine as rhythm, you need to personally experience the cosmic rhythm of your own pulsating Consciousness. Through practice of mantra, visualization and personal reflection, your thinking can become truly vibrant. When Consciousness becomes vibrant, you become vibrant throughout your entire body. You may feel there is a new being within you and that many of the old obstacles simply fall away.

Can the vibrant, activated Consciousness within us also be perceptible, especially when we start to ask: What is the guru within? What is the Light within? What is the innate Buddha?

What is the kingdom of God within? How can we get to know that thinking being in us? How can we differentiate between it and the intellect, which can perform mental acrobatics but constantly has to revise its findings?

And if we allow the Light within us to shine through, we may radiate that Light out to others, and they will feel drawn to us. Our spiritual thinking has to become part of our Consciousness. Otherwise, we are just intellectually clever, and we end up creating conceptualizations that further armour us and prevent the Light from truly emerging.

When we investigate rhythm, we can see that life is not a straight line, but a wave, with its many ups and downs. But whether up or down, it still has the same life Energy. As human beings we need the impetus to lift out from the down to the up. It does not happen automatically. We have to contribute to it through our attitude, our emotions and our choices. The power of choice must be fully recognized.

Sometimes there can be a wave of bliss, when everything seems wonderful and our happiness can be recognized by others. If there is a Light within, we will express that Light, even if we cannot explain it. Yet nothing is permanent, and we cannot always reside in the bright Light. Sometimes we need a little shade to rest, to balance, before exposing ourselves again to this wonderful radiance of Divine Knowledge, of Divine vibration, so that our Consciousness will vibrate with the Divine rhythm.

Practically speaking, it is important not to make major decisions when we are in the trough of the wave. From the crest, we have a different overview and are not under the pressure of the undertow of our existence.

The rhythmic beating of the physical heart can be felt as

a pulse in different parts of the body. Our mental activity can also be considered a kind of pulsing. When we talk about the pulsing of the body, the pulsing of the heart, the pulsing of the mind, what do we feel and think? What effect does reflecting have on our feelings when we have reached a certain level of spiritual awareness or even when we are just beginning to have that awareness? That awareness will sustain us in our daily life. It has to. We must not separate our daily living, with all its duties, functions and limited choices, from our spiritual awareness. Spiritual awareness must be brought into our daily life if we are to become receptive to the radiance of that Consciousness that is pulsing with Divine vibrations.

We do not need to convert from one religion to another, but rather we have to convert the darkness held in our hearts into the Light and vibration of love.

IN THE STRUGGLE to control emotions that can be on the rampage, the heart is sometimes described as a cremation ground. The heart is where selfishness, hate, greed and jealousy are burned away so the heart can be filled with Light. It is in the ashes of our illusions that we find truth.

In the heart, we sacrifice whatever prevents the Light from emerging and shining. Even today, there are some yogis in India who visit cremation grounds to meditate on the impermanence of life. My guru did not send me to the cremation ground, but asked me to reflect on my mortality. When I walked up the Ganges, where the river became much narrower, all along the banks I saw many skulls – the remnants of those pilgrims who asked that their bodies be returned to Mother Ganga's holy waters. It made me think: "What if this were the only life I had? What has to die in me so I can be free now, in this lifetime?"

Literally sitting on a corpse will not necessarily bring realization. It takes deeper thinking to understand that what needs to die is our jealousy, revenge, pride, vanity, competition. All of these personality aspects must become the corpse. Then, with the help of the Divine, we can start to see with the Light of understanding and allow the Light of knowledge to emerge.

The heart is the cremation ground, where, for the love of God, we break our attachments and create the willingness to give up our self-will. What we cannot do for love, we cannot achieve by sheer willpower. The heart is the cremation ground where we burn desires and imaginary needs – needs that are often not real, but illusions that we already know will not satisfy us. These are our preferences, our comfort, our attachments that we sometimes do not even know exist.

If we do not let them go voluntarily, the Divine will come along anyway – perhaps in the form of Śiva, the destroyer of obstacles, and burn them away. Or as Kṛṣṇa, the stealer of butter, who will steal away what we like best, as if saying, "No, that is not where you should put your heart." When things are forcibly taken away from us, it should be a sign to start looking more clearly.

When we sacrifice our comfort, we can become independent of comfort and are no longer limited by our need for it. When we sacrifice our opinions, we may find that they were not correct anyway. When we sacrifice what we call our "security" – which, if you look at it closer, may not be real security at all – we can release a powerful Energy that leads to Liberation.

What would it mean to be truly liberated from the

confinement and constriction of selfishness? Is it not selfishness, if left to run freely, that will tyrannize us? Think about the unhappiness and destroyed relationships that arise when selfishness and self-will run rampant. Nothing good comes from it. And yet many people believe their security is in getting what they want. When we burn away selfishness in the cremation ground of the heart, we set ourselves free and set in motion a process of becoming truly human.

So do not hesitate to sacrifice whatever you hold onto tightly in the wrong belief that it is your security. It is not. True security is recognizing that there is a power greater than ourselves that can take care of us. We need to see our own evolution and how we have been cared for, almost step by step, along the way. What is important is to cultivate a commitment to giving back to life and a willingness to see how many blessings life has given us.

The practice of surrender means offering our limited understanding and limited love to the Divine in return for Divine Love.

THE PATH OF THE LIGHT is the path of the heart. It can only be love that brings Light into the heart. What else could it be? We may feel that we cannot love everybody, but we can try to understand others, especially those who give us the biggest problems. By wanting to understand, we nurture a very different attitude toward that person.

Whichever path we are on, we have to carry the Light in our heart, even if it is just a small light. One little candle can light a whole room. From the flame of just one candle or even from the quick flare of a match, there is no longer total darkness. In the same way, we may feel elevated or inspired, but the feeling soon disappears. Yet from that instant of Light, we may see something new and experience the difference between darkness and a brilliant flicker of insight.

Whatever Light we have in ourselves, we have to fan that bit of ember until it grows into a real flame. Often we begin the path of yoga with Karma Yoga – selfless service – for purification. This path leads to the Light of the heart and to kindling the flame of Light and love. We must protect this inner Light and not let anyone extinguish it or damage it. We are the custodians of the Light in our heart as well as the Light in our mind.

In the Christian tradition, the Holy Spirit is the Light of the heart. And what makes us a creation in the image of God? Divine Love, and expanded Consciousness that moves us beyond our little egocentricities and daily cares, beyond the limits we set for ourselves through unproven beliefs, obligations and ideas.

Freedom is very fragile, even the freedom of the renunciate whose aim is to be free of attachments and desires. Freedom is fragile, but at least there is freedom. The path of Light is the path of Liberation. But we have to experiment, we have to undergo the battle to break with traditions in order to know if the Power that created us in the first place will really take care of us. If we do not give people the chance to prove themselves, we do not know the truth about how they will act. If we do not give the Divine a chance, we will never know the Divine.

If we aim for the Most High, it is not easy. If we want the diamond of Higher Consciousness, it costs. There are many different diamonds, but the most expensive is the clear water diamond. It has no flaws. Costume jewellery sparkles too, but you know it is not the real thing. If you can have the real diamond that reflects the light in every facet, why be satisfied with less? Aim for the Most High. Go for the greatest Light. Become Light yourself and bring the Light to others.

The path of the heart is the path of Light, the Light of love and the Light of understanding. Nothing is more important. Perfection is your individual, personal relationship with the Divine, in whatever name and form you have chosen, or as the Light. If you choose the Light as your symbol of the Divine, you must love the Light, as intimately, as deeply and as intensely – much more so – as your very first love. It is your only true love.

Consciousness is without sex
something is latent, not lost
in the recesses of the mind
smoldering ashes still glow
to light a lamp, to find the way
even a small flame overcomes
darkness.

Light is not enough
action must follow
climbing the path.

10 MIND

THE MIND, like Energy itself, cannot be imagined. The mind has no shape or form. It is like electricity that cannot be seen, but can become visible through its manifestations. Mind is just as elusive as love or faith or hope. It cannot really be made visible because it has an innate quality. In an act of kindness, the act itself manifests the emotion that I name "kindness." Kindness is too abstract even to be defined without manifestation, and yet such manifestations of abstract ideas play a great part in the functioning and expression of the human mind.

Even electricity, which is familiar to us, and which we use all the time, still cannot be defined without symbols. In the Eastern teachings, mind is sometimes compared to a lake. When the water is very still, the lake will reflect our image perfectly. The moment the wind blows on the surface, it ripples and distorts the image. Every thought, every slight impression, like the softest of breaths, makes ripples on the lake of the mind, distorting the accuracy of reflection. Perception of the senses, influence of the emotions and quick mental processes make the ripples. It takes a fraction of a second to assess if we should open or close our eyes, say yes or no, be happy or unhappy. The originating motivation for making those decisions can be traced to our need to survive. Danger is assessed very quickly.

Reason and logic try to make situations predictable, but many situations in life are unpredictable. The incredible power of the imagination is also unpredictable. If several people hear the same word, the image created in each person's mind in response to that word will be different. If everyone is given the same instructions, their responses will also be different. Imagination is extremely powerful. Observe how, through practices such as chanting, you can still the ripples on the lake of the mind and how you can reflect most accurately what is going on in your mind.

Clarify what you mean when you say the word "mind." What are the characteristics, the abilities, the powers of your mind? We all know that we can think, we have memory, we dream, we have conversations in our mind, we can calculate and manipulate. But while we can list our mental abilities, most people only know them superficially. We do not know how we can use the mind fully. We may not have considered that there are more powers available to us than we have realized.

What is intelligence? Can you develop your intelligence? Is developing intelligence only an academic pursuit, or can you train your mind to be more perceptive, sharper, more understanding? How do you use memory? Can you develop memory? Is intuition related to intelligence, and can you develop intuition? In other words, can you actively cooperate with your evolution instead of leaving it to chance? Can you take matters into your own hands and direct your life?

It is sometimes said, "It's all in your mind," or, "Just get it out of your mind." But unless you are given specific directions for how to start, how to observe the rising of emotions clouding the otherwise quite clear perception of the mind, you are no better off. You may intellectually understand what should be done to restrain emotional reactions, but not how to put the understanding into practice.

How much mental energy is channeled into emotions? How much is the will part of the mind? In the practice of yoga, we discover a constant interplay of forces.

What if the function of the human mind were purely the electrical discharge of the brain? What would be the connection between that electrical discharge, the imagination and our sense of identity? Again we are caught in an interplay of forces – the brain matter, the electrical-chemical reaction, the space-time relationship, our sense of identification, the power of emotions and imagination and the influence of change. By *change,* I also mean the influence of death.

What starts to become apparent is that there is a non-material part of us. How can it be "a part" if it is not material? This apparent contradiction is due to the limitation of language. When we start to explore the inner world and inner space, just as in our explorations of outer space, I think we will have to develop some completely new words that may have no root in modern or ancient languages.

YOGA IS A PATH of liberation. Liberation means to be free from all that holds us bound. Up to a point, we survive with the help of the monkey mind – the restless mind that jumps from one thing to another – and so we put our trust there. But if we truly trusted that monkey mind, we would not be concerned with spiritual life at all. Something within us knows there is more.

At first, we need help because we do not have enough discrimination and awareness to use our own power wisely. We are like sleepwalkers that need to wake up. In ordinary life, we often do not notice the succession of happenings that lead to a result, but if we enhance our sense of observation, we can see that nothing happens without due preparation. Part of the learning is to train the mind to accept the facts as they are, without the emotional colouring that wants to see them differently.

Most people carry around the heavy burdens of emotional pain – resentment, dashed hopes, revenge, bitterness – emotions that have not yet been refined. These emotions are a dangerous starting point to set the developing powers into motion. We have to lay a foundation in our lives; otherwise, we become confused. The mental and emotional garbage has to come to the surface and be dealt with. This is the process of character-building, which is essential for any spiritual path no matter what name we give it. The first cakra is pure Energy. What are you going to do with it?

As we gradually gain some understanding and control of the mind through reflection and spiritual practice, we can ask: What more is there to be discovered? What is the potential of the mind?

THE MIND has extraordinary, mysterious powers, but to reach those powers we first need to acknowledge the mental powers that we already have. Most people do not even consider *how* they think. Do you know where the Energy comes from to think? How do you use Energy to think and how much Energy is used? How can you increase that Energy? When you have a thought, how do you use Energy to process that thought into words? Converting Energy to thought and thought into words is all related to vibration.

The process of developing the powers of mind is similar to learning to write. We start by learning the alphabet, then gradually build our vocabulary and understanding of grammar. Eventually we write sentences and short stories. We may dream of writing novels or poetry, but if we have not gone beyond the rudimentaries, it is just wishful thinking. We have to gain a sensitivity toward the language that will allow our style to develop. It is the same with the powers of the mind. We become involved in a gradual process of learning. Some people may take bigger leaps, but they probably accomplished many steps in previous lives and the memories are slowly surfacing. The emotional, human aspect does not allow too large a resurgence of memory because we could not deal with it.

When the mind goes beyond its recognized and known limitations, these powers are considered supernatural or psychic phenomena. What we think are supernatural powers of the mind may be quite natural, but cannot be explained in the usual terms. In yoga, psychic phenomena are considered simply super-sensitivities of a sense. There is a sharpening of perceptions to a heightened state by completely shutting out the usual merry-go-round of thoughts that constantly interferes.

When, after some training, you have learned to listen with your inner ear and see with your inner eye, what you can attain is indeed remarkable. You can develop these abilities through your own efforts. In India I have witnessed the powers that self-mastery and self-discipline bring, and they exceeded my wildest dreams. The first step is becoming aware. Psychic powers may not be easily comprehensible, but the average person cannot even understand the scientific definition of "matter" in the natural world. What we think of as the physical, tangible, solid world is not physical at all, but is a dance of electrons, particles and waves.

When investigating the mind, it is helpful to have healthy doubt – a questioning for the sake of knowing more. It comes back to the practice of awareness – we want to know as much as possible about what is going on. The more we know about our mind, the less we fool ourselves unnecessarily. We probably cannot avoid being fooled until we gain true knowledge based on personal experience. But we can be as aware as possible of what is taking place within the mind and where the mind extends. We want to maintain a heightened awareness. This can be done even though it requires a long, arduous training. If we increase the rate of our thought vibrations safely and in a disciplined way, our mind can do much more than we think it can. But we have to stop being a victim of the sometimes very dynamically active forces, whether negative or positive, destructive or elevating.

What is the mind really capable of? Women can create false pregnancies based on an intensity of desire. People with incomplete brains can function normally. How can we investigate and understand these mysteries? We have telescopes that allow us to see into space and rockets for traveling into space. Can the mind that invented and developed these tools also be capable of much more? I met my guru, Swami Sivananda, in meditation when he was 12,000 miles away. How can this be explained? By his projection and by my receptivity. Can we learn to use our minds to make a connection with someone, when they need help or are in pain? We usually try to project an image of ourselves in the best possible way to be acceptable, to be liked. But if we take the power out of the ego, we can become invisible. We can project Light.

Is the mind capable of exploring more than the three dimensions that we can measure on the material plane? In the practice of Kuṇḍalinī Yoga, the lowest cakra is said to be the source of Energy and power. The second is the seat of imagination and ideas. And the third, in which the emotions reside, is like the kiln where the heat and intensity of the emotions give shape and form to the idea or image. But it starts with pure Energy. We can see Energy at work all around us. If all the Energy comes from one source, who makes the divisions?

What is the original mind? What do we do with this beautiful mind that is basically colourless or contains all colour? Pure mind – no thoughts, no competition, no scheming – is pure Energy. From the centre of Energy it radiates in all directions.

PART FOUR

FINDING THE HIDDEN PLACE

With greater awareness
comes luminous wisdom
this experience beautiful
and frightening at the same time.

The mind dazzled by supreme ecstasies
refuses to return to a dark
and deceitful world with all
those illusions ending in pain.

Passionate desire for awareness
to be again absorbed in the
splendour of Divine Light
I find the secret place on the moon.

11 HIDDEN PLACE

IN THE EASTERN TEACHINGS, mind is sometimes compared to the moon that has no Light of its own, and the source of infinite Wisdom is compared to the sun. The mind, like the moon, can reflect Light, but the reflection is only visible at certain times. When we understand that mind can reflect Light, the practice of reflection – looking deeply within ourselves and asking important questions, such as: Who am I? What is the purpose of my life? – will slowly reveal to us the way. Looking into the mirror of the mind, as into a clear mountain lake, ask: What am I reflecting?

Just as the moon can reflect only part of the sun, the human mind can reflect only part of Divine Wisdom. It would be presumptuous to think that the little moon, however reflective, can hold all of the light of the sun, all of the wisdom of the universe. The mirror reflects without error or missing details, yet the reflection cannot convey the special emanation of the original. And sometimes we are turned away from this Light and do not know it is there. We have to go in search of it.

The Light of Consciousness reflects on the mind when the mind is receptive. Each mind, like each moon, also moves differently and has its own dark spots. Where can the Light be absorbed? What will bounce off and be lost? What does the mind attend to? What does the mind absorb? Even enlightened persons may be quite different from each other because the human mind will always taint what it perceives based on its previous experiences. The need for interpreting what we experience is very powerful.

There is a central place in the mind, symbolically the centre of the moon, a place so hidden it is rarely discovered, a place where Divine Wisdom and Light are absorbed. This hidden place of the mind is the heart of reflected knowledge, the vessel of immortal nectar, the seat of enlightened Consciousness.

To reach the hidden place of the mind requires piercing the darkness of ignorance through searching out the meaning of special dreams and preparing ourselves through the power of the mantra. These practices help us find the path that will lead to that hidden place. It is hidden because our ignorance, our self-deception and false beliefs in the powers of the mind, such as intellect, have kept the Light from our awareness. And yet something in us does know it is there.

When you approach the entrance to the hidden place, it is dark and frightening because it is unknown. A guardian stands at the gate – a big dragon – that will battle you with a thousand doubts. This is the intellect that will fight tooth and nail because it does not want to be defeated under any circumstances, and it knows that spiritual experiences will defeat it. Do you want to give victory to the intellect? By becoming aware and watching other people, you can see that in the end the intellect will let you down. The intellect has a purpose but it is not the Divine in you. You can use the intellect to bring the Light to the surface through practising awareness, but the intellect is only a tool. The power beyond intellect is an intelligence of a very different kind.

If you are sincere and cooperate with your own evolution, at some point you will discover this hidden place in your own mind. Extraordinary experiences will occur when Consciousness is experienced as vibration and the vibrations are allowed to accelerate, leaving behind the dross. Insight and compassion are reflections of this Light.

You are approaching the Divine in yourself, your own essence. The Light in us is like a little grain of rice, not all of the rice in the world. But it gives us a taste. It is like a drop from the ocean, not all of the ocean. But in that drop are the same combination of elements as in the whole. Our Consciousness is like a drop of Cosmic Consciousness. As human beings, we have a desire to return to the source, to the ocean of Light. Each of us travels by different means. The vehicle is of our own making, fired by desire, fired by illusions, fired by a powerful determination to find out, to know, to get there.

To find the entrance
to that hidden place
will demand mental acrobatics
taking risks, destroying concepts
and unproven beliefs
conquering fear of falling from
the rainbow into abyss.

12 THE ENTRANCE

THE MIND IS CAPABLE of reflecting the Light, but it has
to be trained to do so by focus, by discipline, by concentration.
When the mind is intensely focused, there is no Energy left
for distraction. When we are free from being needed, heard,
seen and loved, we can open to higher perceptions and step
into greater freedom. Achieving single-pointed concentration
does not require a belief in a Divine Power. It is rather
approaching a super-conscious state where we become receptive
to knowledge beyond the logical mind, knowledge that we did
not have access to before. Single-pointedness can be achieved

through intention and practice or it can be achieved through danger, pain and fear. The results will be the same.

Scientists may reach single-pointed concentration by constant repetition of experiments. All thoughts, expectations and hopes become geared toward results. Sleep and meals may be forgotten in pursuit of the goal, until finally the scientist gives up, thinking, I've tried everything. At the moment when the mind has run dry and can no longer speculate, insights arise. Two things have taken place – intense concentration, which is needed to create a mood of receptivity, and admitting that the intellect can go only so far. When we acknowledge defeat, we are saying that we need something beyond our own power. When we no longer rely on what we think we know, something else can happen. We can say that the ego-mind is defeated or that the insight comes from a higher level of our own mind. But obviously, the part of the mind we usually depend on cannot provide the answers.

The yogi also uses repetition to become single-pointed and receptive, for example, by repeating a mantra with awareness. If I repeat a mantra with a definite determination to achieve a certain result, I will do it until I achieve that result. If I know that others before me have attained Realization through the mantra, I will be encouraged, which helps to create a receptive mood. The repetition of a mantra is not done automatically. We follow the instruction to observe the mind and its struggles and the impasses and how the impasses arise, how the mind goes into the impasse and comes out of it. By doing this, we increase our sense of observation so we do not have to repeat the same problems. We anticipate them.

The nature of single-pointedness of mind is one thought exclusive of all others. Keeping the mind focused is the process of getting there. When we do acquire knowledge by personal experience, we can pass on the methods to others so they can duplicate the experiment. Gurus have always known how to transmit knowledge. Just because there is not yet scientific evidence of such transmission does not mean that the required mental powers do not exist, only that science has yet to discover the way to measure such power.

MY EXPERIENCE was that it took a long time before I was able to recite even one line of mantra without any interfering thought. Because nobody can see what goes on in your mind, you can cheat yourself very easily by saying, "Oh, this was too faint to be a thought." But if you are determined to know whether something valuable can be gained through the practice, you will be ready and willing to do it honestly.

When you try to direct your thoughts, and other thoughts intrude, the Energy is divided – here is what I want to think, and here is what actually comes through. If you can stop the influx of "other" thoughts, then all the Energy is directed. And that is when things begin to happen. The concentrated mind extends beyond its usual limitations to a much greater capacity. But if your focus stays only on the physical, the mantra will not necessarily help you develop. If that were so, then every opera singer would have attained Higher Consciousness. So obviously something else must be involved.

What is that something else? First, it is preventing intruding thoughts from using part of the Energy. Then it is focus. Sounds are vibrations, but unless you maintain your focus, these vibrations will not take you where they could. Where do you want to go? What do you want to achieve?

Concentrating for three minutes is said to be the first stage of *samadhi*. You could test this hypothesis: Is that possible? Or what if your hypothesis was to find other places from which Wisdom radiates? Could you find one of those places within your own mind? Or perhaps you want to reach another dimension. You may not achieve your goal completely, but even the attempt could be quite interesting. If the brain is like a car and the mind is like the driver of the car, you may examine the hypothesis that the mind can leave the brain just as the driver can leave the car. Or to use another analogy, can the mind emanate from the body like the fragrance that emanates from a flower? If your focus is to be absorbed in the inner Light and finally to become Light, that sets your direction. It is right motivation if you have a deep desire to be in the Light.

Whatever can be described is only the process – the practices set out by those who have achieved their goal and have attained the inner Light. When you become aware that others have achieved this extraordinary goal, you might be inspired to try the same method. Can you get the same result? When you want to duplicate an experiment, you have to observe all the intricate single steps and take them. Some steps cannot be changed or skipped to suit yourself. Only when you have attained results may you discover a way to speed up the process. Speeding up is only possible when there is less resistance. When resistance, which is also Energy, is dissipated, that Energy becomes available to you.

As you test your hypothesis, you may come close to your first destination and experience exhilaration. But you may also be gripped with fear because you are entering unknown territory. You may question: Is my mind sound? Can I think straight? Do I still understand ordinary things that I have understood before? Only repetition will take away the fear. Resistance disappears because you know now that you can "get there." In other words, you can overcome your identification with yourself as the image in the mirror.

Another problem may arise, which is the mental capacity of doubt. The intellect will say that whatever you experience beyond its limitations is an illusion. As the experience is repeated, each time you move one increment closer, until finally you move past the guardian at the entrance of the hidden place of the mind. Then you will become aware that the intellect, although it has quite some power, does not have unlimited power. If it did, it would not need to fight. The next step is to decide to use the intellect for discrimination. Question the doubt itself: Why are you doubting? Perhaps because no one else can confirm exactly what you have experienced; or nobody would believe your experience; or you, yourself, may not accept the experience and question your own sanity. All of these ideas can underlie doubt. The power of doubt rests with pride.

What this really means, in terms of spiritual practice, is to persist. Keep a close record and you will see many repeating patterns. In time, you will learn to master your states of mind, just as you can wake up from a fearful dream. Eventually you will reach that sublime state where you recognize it does not matter if it is day or night, the mind is always dreaming.

When you go past the dragon – the resistance, doubt, pride and egocentricity – you may reach that hidden place in your own mind. You did not know it existed. And as with many things in life – such as vitamins, the division of red blood cells and white blood cells – they have always existed, but we had to discover them and learn the secrets of their functioning.

The same principle can be applied to the mind. When you discover the existence of this hidden place, you strip away the mystery and diminish fear, which eats up Energy. You diminish resistance, which also eats up Energy. And you become much more aware.

When you come to this place, you now enrich yourself with totally new material. Imagine going into outer space for the first time. You would be in awe because you had not known exactly what to expect. You would have speculated, but you would not have known for sure. You would have made many assumptions, based on imagination. Now you may find that some of what you imagined has proven true, while you have to totally discard other preconceptions. The journey to the far reaches of the mind is actually the very same. You may have heard about higher states of Consciousness and people who are enlightened, so you drew conclusions – wrongly or rightly – and created your own hypothesis. Now you may be on the edge of finding out.

You reach the first point of your destination. Although I say "first point" – it may all be there. It is like space with all the stars and planets. Everything exists and is there to be discovered, but we can only go so far in our first explorations. Just as the first major voyages in space were to the moon, our first exploration is to the hidden place in our mind, which reflects the Light of Divine Wisdom. We cannot take all the Light at once. We must take it in degrees. We may have a great flash, but it is a flash, and will not stay.

The more you overcome the resistance of the intellect, the more often you can connect to this place of Light. As you make repeated visits, you may discover new laws, like physicists who discover the laws of the physical world or biologists who understand the laws of nature. You may not give this law a name or define it, but it is there. You will also experience the repercussions of your discovery, which will reshape your entire perspective.

But you cannot stop there, just as astronomers do not stop exploring space once they have reached the moon, but want to know about the sun and other stars, and beyond the known stars and into previously unseen galaxies. What are the possibilities? We can always discover more, but we can never discover it all. Still, the journey of discovery alone will provide an expanded perspective that changes your view of your capabilities.

Your illusory power
changes its own creation
moment by moment.
So, what is real?

Are these dazzling plays inviting
my emotions, or do they
reinforce the mind's fireworks?

Mind alone creates those
dreams, mind is the
dreamer.

13 DREAMS

CONCENTRATION AND FOCUS are one way to access the messages from the hidden place of the mind. Working intensely with dreams is another way. Dreams and their message can be taken as a reality of the inner being that is slowly uncovered through practice – training the mind to remove its blocks. Some dreams may be dramatic or shocking, so that you almost dare not write them down. But if you do, you will get the message very clearly without error. You will not have to search intently for a possible interpretation.

In dreams, images emerge from the unconscious and from

these images we can gather information, receive directions and sometimes even predictions. All the different forms of dreams are created by the mind. The mind functions under many influences.

The side of the mind that is unknown to us is like the dark side of the moon. Dreams from this area bring not just psychological insights but spiritual insights and connections. To experience the hidden meaning of dreams, an intense commitment to the pursuit of awareness is needed. Certain types of dreams will occur only when we have developed a strong degree of surrender, receptivity and intuition. By practising renunciation, we free ourselves from possessiveness that prevents intimate contact with the inner Light.

To prepare yourself, you need to practise surrender to the Divine Will, not try to determine what the Divine Will should be. Because everything is subject to interpretation, tainted by our experience, concepts and cherished beliefs, and coloured by emotions, the work is to get clear, to prepare and to be receptive. Then wait.

I differentiate between ordinary dreams and *dream experiences*, which are spiritual experiences in the dream state. When I recognized that what I loosely termed my "sleep" was really a different state of mind, and "dream" was often a meditative experience, I asked myself how I could help other people attain this same state. In "dream experiences" I am asleep but I am not asleep. The intellect is asleep, so it cannot object or fight. It cannot deny. Therefore the experience is not lost.

Dream experiences prepare the mind to accept something which the intellect fears. The dream experience can be thought of as a way of slipping past the dragon of intellect, which cannot object or defend when it is sleeping. The innate spiritual power in us generates devotional longing and prepares the place in the heart. Then the experiences can be received and understood.

Only when waking consciousness with its limited awareness comes back do the doubts and questions return: "Yes, it would be nice, but…" Then comes the assessment, "Probably just wishful thinking."

When you have a dream or visionary experience of the Divine, you need to know whether the mind has manufactured it or whether it is a true experience. If you have a very elated feeling, and if you cannot reproduce the experience again by your own imagination, you have two clues. You can repeat experiences created by your own imagination, but the real experiences and that feeling of elation you cannot repeat. Yet, when the mind is in the "twilight state," an in-between state where it is open and receptive but also suggestible, you still have to ask: "How do I know for sure?"

You can wait until you receive a confirmation, which may not be absolute proof. Dreams cannot be repeated like scientific experiments. But if you receive something tangible related to the dream, you have evidence that is at least convincing to your own mind. You may dream that a particular gift is coming your way. If you receive that gift in waking life, the dream is confirmed and you have the best evidence that the mind did not create a fantasy. Not every dream needs a confirmation but enough do so that you can tell the difference between an intense dream that was powered by the ego, and one that was truly influenced by the Divine.

The evidence makes the dream experience or vision more convincing to the mind for a longer period of time. We can interpret dream experiences as an interplay of love between the Divine forces and the individual.

An exclusive focus on the Light is necessary to have a dream experience. These experiences happen when the mind is filled with a yearning to be receptive to whatever comes from the Divine Source. The body is in a relaxed state. The mind is not elaborating or monitoring. From my observation, most dream experiences occur around dawn. The degree of relaxation, of letting go, is very important. You can turn the dream state into a fountain of knowledge.

Falling asleep with the mala in your hand, with the thought of Light, imagining a spiral of Light, or filling yourself with Light – all these methods will eventually produce very different dreams. Holding the Light during sleep is one of the key instructions for Dream Yoga. How can you do this? By becoming very familiar with the Divine Light Invocation and by exercising your ability to visualize the Light. Being able to maintain contact with the Light during sleep requires rigorous practice on a daily basis. Eventually, through this regular practice, the power will become more steady.

Bring in the mantra as your last thought in the period immediately before falling asleep. When the self-generating power of the Light mantra is achieved, it can be extended into sleep. When the body is filled with Light during sleep, contact with the Divine essence is maintained. Dreams arising from this state are intuitive illuminations, expressing a forgotten truth or revealing a truth that has moved away from our awareness into a far distance. If we brush aside these dreams, we deprive ourselves of an understanding of Consciousness.

Dreams can reveal to us events back to the time of birth, but they can also take us back to the time before birth.

Where was I before I was conceived? What is this "I" that has manifested again, and for what purpose? Lost memories of past lives can be recovered through dreams. They may come in a condensed version to reveal something of great importance for our further development.

The twilight language of the mind tries to convey something to us, hoping that we will eventually want to know. When we approach dreams without judgement, without assessment, but questioning, "What is possible?" many levels of reality can be uncovered. Some dreams may come to indicate that something beyond the ordinary is going to happen. These types of dreams can prepare us to accept without questioning how it is possible or how the mind enters into it or can hold onto it. These experiences also help us recognize how much patience the Divine exercises. When we gain access to the unknown hidden place of the mind, we realize that we are part of the Divine, just as the drop is part of the ocean.

THE IDEA OF DREAMING itself has to be thoroughly investigated. While we sleep, mental activity carries on even if we cannot recall the activity, such as when we are in deep sleep. But there is never a total cessation of the activity in the mind. All activity of the mind leads back to the same Energy, which just varies in strength, in speed and in the range of vibration. Consciousness is vibration. Thinking is vibration. Our voice is vibration. The Energy to think, to remember, and to express thoughts is all the same Energy, just at a different rate of vibration.

Māyā, which is connected to the hidden meaning of dreams, is also vibration – vibrations of very powerful illusions.

But some illusions are closer to the truth than we acknowledge. Are dreams illusions? Even if they are, by exploring them we can begin to understand and recognize certain interactions to which we would otherwise have no access. Māyā provides the illusions that eventually can manifest in a way that will allow us, through awareness, to recognize the Light that is also within illusions. At that moment, the projections of Māyā are removed and the extraordinary contents of dreams can become a reality.

The sphere of light is growing larger and larger
and brighter and brighter
like a thousand suns.
The light streaming forth leaks through
the clouds of the mind
creating a beautiful disk, Divine Mother
in its centre.

My eyes are absorbed in Her beauty.
My mind becomes intoxicated
by those streaming rays of brilliant white light.
I command my mind to remember all and
everything
to indulge just for a brief moment, just once
with all its power
to recall the smallest detail.

14 VISIONS

WISDOM DOES NOT DROP fully formed from heaven. We would not be prepared for it if it did. There has to be a way to open the mind, to take away fear and hesitation and to refine the imagination. If the mind fantasizes in the hope or desire to have contact with the very best in oneself or to take another step toward this greater power, the mind will eventually become strong enough to receive something that it would otherwise be afraid of.

Any visionary experiences we have through our efforts are not necessarily given in a final form. They demand clarification.

To help us understand, perhaps we have to translate the experiences into words. But we must refrain from an immediate assessment, and also from a greed to have it all when we can only deal with a little. The visions that come from focusing on the Light are of a mystical nature. They come from the Light. Visions are mystical experiences of the Light, but only if they influence us to a new, different way of living, thinking and acting. We slowly begin to realize that to become receptive to Divine revelation, we first need to develop intense focus and surrender. Then the language of the Divine echoes within us, eventually reminding us of our Divine origin.

Mind and emotions can be very positive and can facilitate a spiritual experience, but they can also be destructive and interfere with it. There is an interplay of forces, and only surrender to the Divine will give us the necessary control. When we can surrender, it contributes to the recognition of the Divine and the existing images in the mind, and brings them together. If we can avoid concretizing our ideas and impressions, we can shift our focus like we do in a dream. Then very subtle images can emerge.

Images can be very fleeting and often not completely formed. Before an image can be held in the mind's eye, it may already be gone. In a visionary experience the form can be rather ethereal, which makes it difficult to describe in a way that is understandable, even to ourselves. Sometimes it may be more a feeling or a very brief flash, like lightning, sometimes even a single image or one word. We have to see what emerges rather than demanding definiteness.

When we are able to still the emotions, we can let the subtle images surface and look at them. When we are receptive, we can receive tremendous insights and answers to questions of lifelong importance. When we are in touch with this knowledge, we feel very enriched and elated. We may have a feeling of: "Oh, *that's* what it is!" And yet if somebody asks you, "Well, what is it?" you would have to resort to silence because you could not really answer. It is a different kind of knowing, which the intellect cannot grasp or explain. And if we can keep all interferences out, we will internalize the experience and bring about great changes in ourselves.

Even if the knowledge is tainted by the colour of our personalities – that colour being the result of the accumulated human experience of each of us – nevertheless, it is still possible to be receptive to knowledge radiating from other sources beyond the limited knowledge of our own minds. The mind may have to struggle to try to verbalize what it has experienced. Great difficulties putting the experience into language is an indication that the knowledge came from beyond the mind.

When we are elevated and contact this inner Light, some of our most troubling personality aspects seem to disappear without a struggle. We cannot help but look in wonder at what this Energy can do with the tools of body, mind and senses. It is as if someone has saved our life. The natural response would be to thank them profusely and ask what we could do in return. Can you feel the same way toward the Divine in yourself that tries to lift you out of your mental confinement?

It is essential to surrender to the high quality of spiritual Energy that has helped uplift you. To stay connected with the spiritual experience, reflection is necessary – reflection in a state of relaxation and surrender. You can just accept what happens, almost like an onlooker. When you close your eyes, you can recall the fullness again. You cannot repeat the actual experience, but you can reflect on a beautiful memory and allow a feeling of wonder.

The Light is diffuse. You can unscrew a light bulb and hold it in your hands, but you cannot grasp the light itself. You may have a beautiful experience where you know "I am not the body and I am not the mind." The mind becomes only a witness when you experience yourself as Light.

The validity of any experience depends upon what you do with it. If, even for a short time, you have come "face to face with God," as the Christian teachings describe it, you will never be the same again. A beautiful transformation will take place. The transformation is not sudden and does not proceed automatically. The effects can even disappear if you do not clear the channel for higher inspiration, which means building character and developing self-mastery. It takes time, training, effort, patience and persistence.

IF YOU HAVE AN EXPERIENCE of the Light and the experience fades, it is a mistake to think that the Light has disappeared. You have just experienced the presence of Light for the limited time that awareness is heightened. When you concentrate on something, it does not mean that you can retain concentration for twenty-four hours. But when you are intensely concentrated, you attain a certain state of awareness.

Energy is perceived only when it manifests, but when Energy is not perceived it does not mean it is not there. So we cannot say there is ever an absence of Energy or an absence of Light. What makes Light absent is only our ability to perceive it. It is the same with many things – they exist but we need to discover them, which is why awareness is so tremendously important. When we discover something new, it is only new to us because through our lack of awareness we have not discovered it before.

The absence of Light, then, is only apparent. The absence is due to ignorance, or an absence of awareness, or a failure to think in depth. It is very important to understand that when Energy manifests, even in the human mind, it is constantly fluctuating and thereby creates an interplay of its own forces. All spiritual experiences have a limited lifetime because of this fluctuation. Awareness will increase in some areas and then apparently decrease, but only apparently.

Memory is essential, but memory of an experience cannot be taken for the experience itself, even though the feeling of re-experiencing may be present. Putting things into the memory bank is very helpful. It is like collecting spiritual capital that will result in benefits at later times when awareness temporarily dims. Sometimes awareness dims to the point where everything we remember is doubted. Then the interplay of forces can be particularly devastating, especially if your intensity of desire for the Light is diminished.

Being in the Light is like being in the sun. At one point, we will want to step into the shade. But that does not mean the Light is lost. The mind just needs a chance to recover. When it has renewed itself through this period of rest in the shade,[1] the cosmic dance can start anew. Life is not a straight line, but a wave. It is important to pay attention to momentum, so we can rise to the crest of the wave once again, and again, and again.

---

1   Mantra for the Manipura Cakra: "In the Manipura of yours I serve Him as a dark cloud, which is the only refuge (of the world) raining down the rain on the three worlds scorched by the sun that is Hara. (This cloud which) carries the rainbow, Indra's bow, bedecked with ornaments of various glittering jewels, and which has flashes of lightnings due to His Śakti bursting forth from the enveloping darkness (of the cloud)."

PART FIVE

ECHOING
BACK

The word of the Divine
is only heard when silence
pervades the mind,
even the mantra will not reign.

Breath is flowing gently
filling the cave of the heart
ready to receive Her divine word.

15 LANGUAGE

WE CAN HAVE SPIRITUAL EXPERIENCES that are linked either to sound through language, or to sight, like the great visionaries. To be receptive to those very fine waves of vibration of Cosmic Energy, our perception has to be refined. Divine experiences are not given in a final form, but demand clarification and must first be translated into words for our own understanding.

A question then arises about the nature of language. Before recorded history, language already existed. Written language was a later development. The spoken word is sound and sound is vibration. If you translate your experience into the vibration of the voice through the spoken word, and if you retrace the steps backward again – the spoken word, the experience, the essence of the experience, the perceived vibration – can the entire Cosmic Energy be put into one factor, that everything is vibration? The more clear your own perception is – which does not mean good or bad, but means without overlay of concepts, opinion, convictions, beliefs – the more you will be able to perceive what really is.

Is there or has there been a language (I have to use the term "language" for lack of a better word) of the unconscious and the super-conscious? Is it different from language as we generally think of it? Is there a language beyond the human level and are there other sources not easily accessible to human beings unless they have developed this highly sensitive perception?

There are many ways of communication and if we investigate beyond those already known, we can explore not only how specific types of dreams occur that are really spiritual experiences, but also the spiritual aspects of the whole Kuṇḍalinī system beyond the first three cakras, which means from the Heart Lotus upward. This means going beyond the survival level to a more compassionate, elevated state of being.

We can gather thoughts that reveal something forgotten, for which language does not have a precise word. Often this is expressed as revealing the truth, but what is meant by truth? Is everything else false? Everything has a reality at its own level and therefore is not necessarily false or an untruth. It is just that many things are a process toward another reality, for which the word "truth" is not a good equivalent.

When I converse in my own mind with the innermost level of myself, which is not to be mistaken for the psychological level, I am involved in a kind of communication beyond words. Something in me knows that I have experienced on a deeper level. What is revealed is not so much the greater truth as it is my ignorance. By having revealed to myself my ignorance, I become free to understand something that has always been there – that which is and always has been. So I reveal to myself my resistance, my ignorance, and maybe my lack of depth, while approaching from a faint inner knowing that there is something beyond.

In the Eastern scriptures, there is an idea expressed that those who are devoted to the Divine will not come to harm. If I have not revealed my ignorance to myself, I may take this statement literally and think, "Nothing can harm me. I won't get sick. I won't get a cold. I will never lose a job. I will not lose money because I'm a devotee and no harm will come to me." It depends on how I define "harm." But if I reveal my own limitations to myself and venture out from the literal, I will know that even if I end up with a life-threatening or debilitating disease that harms my body – I will still not lose contact with the Divine.

All I have to do is remove the garbage, which is really the ignorance, and also surrender to the fact that there is ignorance. If another emotion, like pride, comes in and says, "I may not know everything, but I think I understand quite well," then the question is, "Do I?" To think we have arrived is the first step of ignorance. By recognizing that there is never a time when we have arrived, we can remove the ignorance and something else can come in. Renunciation is often described as a very difficult, strong discipline. But renouncing, if approached in the right way, is freeing ourselves to allow something greater to be experienced.

On the human level, how can you become aware of communication that is just on the border of words – when you feel, "Yes, I know what you mean, but I, too, cannot put it into words"; where there is an exchange of perception and influence? The major way is to allow intuition to come into full bloom. It is intuition that overcomes ignorance and will clear the way for accurate perception.

If a friend tells me something very sad, very dramatic, she can have several motivations. She may want to talk about it to unburden herself. She may want to receive some comfort. She may want to gain some understanding for future interactions. If I want to understand why she tells me what she does, I have to listen to her with intuition, being sensitive to the fluctuations or the vibration of her voice, and hearing those as much as the words spoken. Then I can respond, not necessarily with words. But if communication exists, she will know she is understood.

These kinds of interactions – being sensitive, listening, hearing beyond the words – are all the forerunners to experiencing the Divine in ourselves. We need to have communication with the Divine within ourselves. We can let our personality aspects get into quite wild talks, accusations as well as self-defence, but we can also have communication with very different personality aspects, such as the ones that say, "I should have been more compassionate. I should have been more patient." Beyond these personality aspects there is another level of understanding that has compassion, but also the knowledge that life's inevitable challenges must be experienced to increase awareness of the Divine within.

But without sensitivity, perception is limited. Until there is the sensitivity to perceive subtle vibrations, you have to work to develop it. The vibration of basic talk and thinking can cancel out the vibration of higher, more refined thinking. Anything gross can subdue what is subtle to a point that it takes another lifetime to recover. How could we perceive the subtle vibration of thinking without having laid a foundation? That is why we start by chanting the mantra out loud. The senses are tuned and the vibrations from the sound can nourish the mind. The subtle vibrations of chanting the mantra in the mind are more easily lost.

If the rational mind can be blocked during spiritual practice, intuition can open us to a new understanding. It is like opening a door. Then speech comes from a different centre – from a place where intuition works with inspiration and with a sense of awe. Poetry can flow from this place. Preparation for opening this door involves an intense desire to know what your life is for and why you are here. Then awareness gradually increases and many old concepts can be discarded.

Just as we can feel vibration in the body from the emotions – there can be times when we literally shake with anger or fear – a different, subtler vibration can be felt from the heart. The vibrations evolve from the more gross to the more subtle. Intuition is a very fine vibration. At some point, when longing is deep, intuitive perception takes over and the contact with the inner Light is made. We are nourished by that experience, yet it also must be kept alive so that desires and attachment lose their grip.

Reflect for a moment. If you can accept the idea of the Light within, why do you think you can? Because you have experienced the Light, even if you have not communicated it to your human mind. But in a moment of receptivity, the fluctuation of the mind was great enough to bring back the memory.

Pay attention to intuitive perceptions, even if they seem cloudy or faint. Make a point of sitting down and reflecting on intuitive insights that come like lightning. The flow of greater Consciousness will sometimes be experienced as the Light of intuition and sometimes like lightning in a flash. Suddenly you understand, as if totally new, something that has always been there. Suddenly you have a flash of insight and wonder where it came from. If you pay attention and try to find out, you can tap into that source of radiating Consciousness. The mind can reflect the Light from this greater source.

Let yourself open up to intuitive experiences. First, because you then invite more. And second, because these experiences will come back in a different way, becoming clearer. There is always a loss in these experiences when they reach consciousness, so if you tell me about a tiny experience and think, "Oh, it's really nothing, I should not even have mentioned it," I know, from my own experience, that your tiny experience was at least twice, if not three or four times as big, but you have not been able to grasp it.

At one point, the larger experience will emerge, if you take time and you are quiet afterward, and if you try to keep from criticizing it, assessing it, conceptualizing it. Just let this memory be. Take it as a whole without breaking it apart. Most experiences are short, like lightning. But if you watch lightning, it is often enough to light up the dark sky, the dark mind.

My understanding is that the language of the Divine *is* present if we allow it to emerge and if we are willing to listen. We need not necessarily be able to communicate our experience to somebody else. And if we can, then not too soon, not before we have understood or allowed it to resonate within ourselves. If the ordinary mind does not meddle by assessing and intellectualizing, the experience will echo back. The voice of the Divine must echo in us. For "voice" you can say "vibration," but the vibrations will have to come to you in a way that you recognize them.

To receive Divine revelation, we must prepare by intense focus and surrender. If you surrender to your mind, you will not be able to get out of that intellectual trap. We have to move into the intuitive, into greater subtlety. Until we become an echo, we will not even know what the Divine is communicating.

The most powerful inner experiences can really only be expressed through symbols, such as Śiva and Śakti. But we have to remember that symbols are not to be taken literally. In the same way, Jesus, the man, does not have the same powerful meaning as the Christ Consciousness of the individual called Jesus. If people focus too much on the personality, they will not develop Christ Consciousness because it never even enters their minds. They have too many preconceived ideas, so intuition cannot be active.

Our Divine origin is so very elusive to the human mind. It can only become stronger when we interact with that inner source, the inner experience, because that is what nourishes, encourages, revitalizes. These are the messages from the hidden place of the mind. Without the inner experience, the source of Light or your own Divine origin is left undiscovered. Then this entire human life would be lost because you would not make contact with this Light of Consciousness.

Energy as such
is neither feminine nor masculine.
It is not good or bad, either.
Application changes
decides on the course of evolution.
Creation, destruction
are just changes of Energy-Vibration.

16 KARMA

WHEN UNMANIFESTED ENERGY is symbolically expressed as Śiva, and manifested Energy is expressed as Śakti, Śiva is shown as physically larger than Śakti. This has nothing to do with human relationships. But each person, male or female, has to realize there is more Energy available than is used, and that *more* Energy can be given the name Śiva to make communication simpler. In our lives, there is never so much manifested as there is Energy available. Through spiritual practices we may discover that we are capable of doing much more and understanding much more than we ever believed possible.

Energy is indestructible. We can change it, but we cannot destroy it. Think of Consciousness as a vortex of Energy that can take different shapes and forms. If we are reborn, that vortex of Energy will take another vehicle. Like a tornado, which you see only because of the dust it collects, the Energy in the vortex collects particles of life experiences. The vortex must have a possibility of memory. Think of how technology has developed to the point where so much data can be stored in a tiny computer chip. This technological development can help us understand how the vortex of Energy called Consciousness can contain everything about ourselves for a future life.

If all the Energy is one, how can it sometimes be positive and sometimes be negative? The power is neutral, but the polarity of the positive and the negative exists within us. Each pole has a different vibration. Is it the fault of the Divine if you are tempted to act against your own principles, or is it your own lack of responsibility for your actions? Most of our actions are based on emotions. If you look at me strangely, I may think, *Oh, she doesn't like me,* and I will retaliate by walking by. I've seen her, but I won't let her know. We are constantly in a struggle of acceptance/rejection within ourselves and within our surroundings. But our choices are our responsibility.

We are surrounded by electricity. The same electricity can power cameras, sound equipment, air conditioners, heaters, computers. It is all electricity and serves us well. We can manipulate it at will. If the electricity is used to electrocute someone, is it the fault of the electricity or of those who use it in that way? Once you begin to understand the neutrality of power, it becomes extremely difficult to avoid responsibilities that you may not even have considered until now.

Karma is action, and action implies cause and effect. When we experience positive effects from our actions, we may feel rewarded, and when we experience negative effects, we may feel punished. But karma is neither punishment nor reward. For example, if in one lifetime we misuse our intelligence, in another lifetime that intelligence may not be available for us. It is not "God" that is punishing us. We are just experiencing the effects from our actions, which eventually come back to us like the echo of our own voice.

On a day-to-day level, karma is positive when the actions we take are not solely for our own benefit to the exclusion of others. Karma is negative when there is exploitation of others for self-gratification. Selfless service can clear up karma that we have created along the way through selfishness and greed. Because we are the doers, we can also undo. And if someone was hurt by our actions, we can undo the effects to a large degree – sometimes through opposite actions, sometimes through asking forgiveness, sometimes through visualizing the person in Light, particularly if the individual is no longer alive.

By being very conscientious and taking time to reflect on the events of our lives, we can assess ourselves and determine to what degree we are satisfied with our actions and in what areas we can improve. We start to see our blind spots. And we understand that because we create the three worlds – the mental world, the emotional world, and the world of our self-created illusions – we also have the power to destroy them.

Karma also means challenges and opportunities. Challenges constantly arise. Many are met and many are not. Those that are not met will come back, like any lesson. Each time we are meeting ourselves, and sometimes we meet our darkest self. But if there is even a glimmer of Light, we can catch a glimpse of our own potential and learn from the challenge. We may think that reincarnation is wonderful because our lives have offered wonderful opportunities. But then we must respond generously to our good fortune by giving back to life and using the Energy to benefit others, rather than exclusively satisfying ourselves.

KARMA CREATED when power has been misused can be remedied. The way to remove this kind of karma is to increase the positive frequency of vibration in our own minds and hearts. We can bring balance through the Light of understanding and through the vibration of our mental activity. We talk in our minds. We have conversations, defend our actions and accuse ourselves. We call this by different names like "guilt" and argue about it. We have a judge that criticizes. These are all aspects of the same Energy used in what we consider a negative way because they do not bring blessings or harmony into our own lives or into the lives of those around us.

Vibrations that emanate from speech, from thought, from emotions are different when they are in harmony. Spiritual practices can bring about these changes in vibrations of emotions. For example, we can calm down anger or even remove anger through chanting mantra. Suffering can also calm us down – but it is a more painful way. Removing our ignorance about suffering, understanding our challenges and acting in proportion to the challenges – all these approaches create a different rate of vibration of both Light and sound within us. We can choose practical exercises to bring the

Light of understanding into action. When our focus on Light intensifies, even the vibration of our voice will change to a more gentle, harmonious one.

If we train the mind to understand and be receptive to the Light and what it really means – not only on an intellectual level, but on a personal level – we create positive vibrations. Ask: How was I created by Divine Light? How can I rediscover this Light in myself? What can I do to discover Light in others? We can think that the Light is residing in us wherever we go, and that there is no place where it would not be. But we may also realize that there is really no place without the vibration of sound. Are they different vibrations – sound and light vibrations? Yes, because they are perceived differently through the human mind. No, when it is realized that they come from the same source. It is similar to water that can crystallize into snow, evaporate into steam and fog, or be fluid and moving. Yet all are manifestations of the same element.

By training the mind to become more flexible, courageous and able to enter realms of thinking that the untrained mind would not dare to attempt, we generate a vibration that will attract others on the same level of development or those who may be more highly evolved. And when we reach a certain point of evolution, we will attain a karmic situation where we contact someone who can help us take the final steps toward Liberation.

Gurus often say that either a student's karmic situation is not ripe enough to accept them as a disciple or it is so ripe that such acceptance is inevitable. But even if accepted, it is not a guarantee of the individual's Liberation because each person determines the intensity of their own pursuit. The magnitude of the help given by a spiritual teacher is very rarely understood. Similarly the magnitude of the gift of life itself is often not recognized.

Is it possible to go beyond karma? Those who have a certain state of Realization naturally will not act in certain ways. For example, they will be free of jealousy and revenge because they have understood interaction, interpenetration, how all things are interlinked. It is possible to remove ourselves from this chain of interaction by developing awareness through lifetimes.

When there is truly a knowing of the oneness of all and a complete surrender to the Divine, we become an instrument of the Divine. When the Divine in us plays the melodies, the instrument itself has no decision-making capacity. But if we have not surrendered, the idea that there is no karma is an illusion.

When the principles of Śiva and Śakti are entirely understood, not intellectually but with your whole being, everything is seen as Divine action, as different frequencies of vibration, which do not create any karma. As an illustration, we can compare an idea to a stone thrown in the water. The stone makes a shallow dent in the water from which waves emanate, becoming weaker and weaker and larger and larger. But the waves are not separate from the water and do not colour it. The waves are not good or bad. In the same way our actions, on the basis of the Śakti principle, are not good or bad; they are relative. The power is neutral. It is rare to be able to see behind the veil of appearances and to accept the vast spectrum of life while understanding it as vibration. If we open to this view, we cannot exclude or judge anyone else differently from ourselves. All are part of the one.

It is through the Light of understanding and the Light of

love that we will grow until eventually we are lifted to a new level of being. When we experience Divine Union – when the drop of individual Consciousness returns to the ocean of Cosmic Consciousness – we are released from the Māyā of our limited understanding.

Beyond Māyā, no karma.

Each life full of challenges and links
in the chain of evolution.
Thoughts arise powerfully.
I am smaller than a grain of sand,
a star in the universe.

17 AN OPEN QUESTION

WE MAY START on the spiritual path with a desire to know and a sense that somewhere there must be a map to greater knowledge. All of the different methods, practices and exercises are like that map to the Light. When we discover the map, we study and train. The greatest teachers can only point the way. We each have to make our own way to arrive at the destination.

In all of us there is something perfect, and what is perfect cannot be improved but only uncovered. Any teacher can only help activate what is already there. Can you activate the best in yourself? Can you uncover the Light within?

It is a process – like exercising to develop more strength

and flexibility or like a seed growing into a tree that will bear fruit. We may already have an inner knowing that the search is worth any effort. Those without that inner knowing will soon give up.

By our own efforts, we develop more of the potential that exists within us. Everything in our lives then becomes a learning experience. Usually we evolve through tragedies and dramas until we start to understand. As we make our way back by slowly learning the painful way, we begin to recognize the facts and to accept them for what they are. One day, the suffering is great enough to wake us up. As human beings, we learn by trial and error. When we wake up and start to see our errors, we also gain compassion and understanding for others.

Through spiritual practices we contact the Light that is indeed ours. It is like washing off the mud of selfishness, self-centredness, self-glorification – letting all that "self" go and becoming selfless. Once we clean up what covers it and come in contact with the hidden place within the mind, the Light will radiate its power. In fact, the Light is the very source of power that keeps us alive. Now this power can emanate brilliantly.

When we discover this place of radiating Light, our world enlarges. We recognize that we are part of the Light and the Light is part of us. In this place, there is nothing superfluous.

IT IS IMPORTANT TO RECOGNIZE that we go through these various stages of development and that we do not have a *total* enlightenment experience all at once because we could not handle it. The experience will emerge in sequences. First something must attract our attention before we see it. Gradually we sense that there is more. Intuitive inspiration or illumination develops over time. And when we truly know something with our intuition, the intellectual part of the mind will no longer be so terribly frightened.

Complete enlightenment or liberation is not as complete as we would like to think. The element of time plays a part. It takes time to be born, to learn, to speak, to walk, to think, to grow up. The word "total" in connection with love, freedom or enlightenment finalizes something that is not final.

Enlightenment is a mystical experience beyond concepts and philosophical speculations. Enlightenment means dying to the world of ignorance and darkness created from our conceptualizations and accumulated ideas. The three worlds – physical, mental and emotional – need to be seen in their limitations as the playground of Māyā. We begin to recognize that there are many more dimensions than the three on which we, as human beings, generally function.

But it is just as difficult for concrete thinkers to go beyond the limits of their mind as it is for the greatest of scientists, who cannot answer the question: Where does the universe begin and where does it end? We know there are millions of galaxies. But within the limitation of three-dimensional thinking, we cannot perceive what is beyond three dimensions. Physicists struggle because they cannot see the smallest of particles; but because they can see the traces, they know there is something. We can create symbols to represent what we cannot perceive with our senses, but we cannot bring down to a three-dimensional level something that does not exist here.

When you are on top of the mountain, cars driving along a freeway look like tiny dots. Can you tell which type of cars they are? How many cylinders they have? How fast they are going? Seen from this perspective, these details are insignificant.

When the mind rises to a new height or moves in a different sphere, everything we have known looks very different, and the concerns from that level do not really matter anymore. We are in a different atmosphere and time frame.

Can you approach the idea that Consciousness is Light that can spin out its worlds like a spider spinning a web, but equally can *absorb* those rays of Light back into its own centre? But as we use language, the words start to create a tangible image again for that which is formless, because if there is a centre there is an exterior, an interior. Language is limiting, which is something we have to accept.

WE CAN COME BACK to the original teachings. Śiva is Energy as such, Śakti is how the Energy is used in thought, in ideas in creation. If there is one source of Energy, it can radiate something very weakly or very strongly. There are different manifestations of that radiation. There is one source that vibrates differently and the different vibrations make the manifestations appear separate.

We have seen that everything in the universe vibrates and changes its frequency and rhythm. We have discovered that we can change certain types of vibrations in ourselves, when we recognize them and gain control over them. We can change our thoughts, our speech, our emotions. But we still have to enter the state beyond mind. What is beyond mind? Asking this question can bring up all of our concepts. You may use what you think you know to develop a hypothesis. Then exert effort to experiment until you find a path that may or may not be workable... that is to be seen.

We can use outer space as an analogy for inner space. To

go into outer space we build all sorts of complicated devices because of the limitations of our bodies' needs. To pierce through the limitations of our mental capacities, we have to access the trustworthy tools of spiritual disciplines. Using these tools together with a powerful desire will help get us there.

We can think of the planet earth and the force fields surrounding it as a metaphor. Symbolically, what would it take for a vortex of Energy at the time of death to pierce through all of the force fields? Perhaps one vortex can go only so far because that is how much power has been developed. In another lifetime it may go further. To go beyond rebirth, you may have to pass beyond all the forces surrounding the planet.

Space flights are just another manifestation of the human desire to break the limitations that have been accepted in the past. We explore the universe to find our place in the universe and the purpose of life. But what are the possibilities of the mind? Our senses can be trained for greater perception. Only those courageous enough to explore and with a passionate desire to know will venture into the unknown. For some, the outer space of the mind is too intriguing to ignore.

What do you do after developing a higher state of Consciousness? What do you do after you have cultivated a talent? That question simply does not occur. A true artist always knows that there is something more to be done – something better, finer, more beautiful, more perfect. Nothing is the best, the last, the finished product.

The entire universe is still an open question.

APPENDIX

THE DIVINE LIGHT INVOCATION

Instructions:

Stand erect, feet shoulder-width apart.

Keep the eyes closed and focus them on the space between the eyebrows.

Lift the arms above the head at the same time as you smoothly and gradually tense the whole body, while you inhale. The arms should be kept straight and the tension maintained throughout the body.

Hold the tension and the breath.

Make the following affirmation to yourself, silently and with all the concentration possible:

I am created by Divine Light.
I am sustained by Divine Light.
I am protected by Divine Light.
I am surrounded by Divine Light.
I am ever growing into Divine Light.

Then slowly lower the arms as you exhale and relax.

Keep the eyes closed and use your imagination to see

fig. 1.

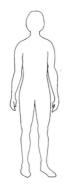

fig. 2.

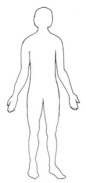

fig. 3.

yourself standing in a shower of brilliant white Light.

See the Light pouring down upon you, flowing into the body through the top of the head, filling your entire being.

Now, without raising the arms, keeping them at your side, tense the body and inhale.

Hold the tension and the breath.

Mentally repeat the Invocation:

I am created by Divine Light.
I am sustained by Divine Light.
I am protected by Divine Light.
I am surrounded by Divine Light.
I am ever growing into Divine Light.

Slowly exhale and relax.

With the arms beside the body, concentrate on feeling a warm glow of Light suffuse your entire body, outside as well as inside.

Acknowledge silently to yourself:

Every cell of this, my physical body,
is filled with Divine Light.
Every level of consciousness
is illumined with Divine Light.
Divine Light penetrates every single cell of my being,
every level of consciousness.
I have become a channel of pure Light.
I am one with the Light.

The Divine Light Invocation is an exercise of will as well as an act of surrender.

Be receptive to the Light and accept that you are now a channel of Divine Light.

Express your gratitude with deep feeling.

Have the desire to share this gift with someone whom you wish to help.

Turn your palms forward.

You can now share the Divine Light with any friend or relative. Keep the eyes closed and visualize him or her standing before you.

Mentally open the doors of your heart centre and let the Light stream forth toward the feet of this person.

See the Light encircling the person and spiraling upward in a clockwise direction, enveloping the body completely.

See the spiral moving high up into the sky, taking his or her image along with it.

Finally the person merges into the source of the Light and becomes one with the Light.

You may even lift your head to follow the spiral of Light, keeping the eyes closed.

When the person has passed from your view, relax and silently give thanks for having the opportunity to help someone in need.

You are now ready to begin all over again, putting others into the Light, one by one, in the same way. As you become more familiar with the Invocation, you may take several people in a group or a family together.

If you should want to help many people, you must repeat the complete Divine Light Invocation as soon as you notice that your attention begins to slacken.

RECOMMENDED READING

SWAMI SIVANANDA RADHA

The Devi of Speech: The Goddess in Kundalini Yoga. Kootenay Bay, BC: Timeless Books, 2005.

The Divine Light Invocation. Kootenay Bay, BC: Timeless Books, 2006.

Kundalini Yoga for the West. Kootenay Bay, BC: Timeless Books, 2004.

Mantras: Words of Power. Kootenay Bay, BC: Timeless Books, 2005.

Realities of the Dreaming Mind: The Practice of Dream Yoga. Kootenay Bay, BC: Timeless Books, 2004.

When You First Called Me Radha: Poems. Kootenay Bay, BC: Timeless Books, 2005.

SIR JOHN WOODROFFE

Garland of Letters. India: Nesma Books, 2001.

Serpent Power. Madras, India: Ganesh & Co., 2000.

Shakta and Shakti: Studies in the Mantra-Śāstra. Madras, India: Ganesh & Co., 1998.

KAŚMIR ŚAIVA TEXTS

Abhinavagupta: A Trident of Wisdom, Translation of Parātrīsikā-Vivarana. Singh, Jaideva. Albany, NY: SUNY, 1989.

The Aphorisms of Śiva (Sivasūtra), with a commentary by Bhaskaracarya. Translated with exposition and notes by Dyczkowski, Mark, S.G. Varanasi, India: Dilip Kumar Publishers, 1991.

The Doctrine of Vibration: An Analysis of the Doctrines and Practices of Kashmir Shaivism. Dyczkowski, Mark S.G. Albany, NY: SUNY, 1987.

Kashmir Shaivism: The Secret Supreme. Lakshman Jee, Swami. Albany, NY: SUNY, The Universal Shaiva Trust, 1988.

The Krama Tantricism of Kashmir: volume 1. 4th edition. Rastogi, Navijan. Delhi: Motilal Banarsidass, 1982.

Pratyabhijñāhrdayam: The Secret of Self-recognition. Singh, Jaideva, Delhi: Motilal Banarsidass.

The Stanzas on Vibration: The Spandakārikā with four commentaries. Translated with an introduction and exposition by Dyczkowski, Mark S.G. Albany, NY: SUNY, 1992.

The Triadic Heart of Śiva: Kaula Tantricism of Abhinavagrupta in the Non-Dual Shaivism of Kashmir. Muller-Ortega, Paul Eduardo. Albany, NY: SUNY, 1989.

The Yoga of Delight, Wonder, and Astonishment: A Translation of the Vijñāna-bhairava with an Introduction and Notes by Jaideva Singh. Albany, NY York: SUNY, 1991.

RESOURCES FOR THE TEACHINGS
OF SWAMI SIVANANDA RADHA

Yasodhara Ashram, yoga retreat and study centre
Box 9, Kootenay Bay, British Columbia, Canada, V0B 1X0
(800) 661-8711
info@yasodhara.org
yasodhara.org

ABOUT THE AUTHOR

SWAMI SIVANANDA RADHA (1911–1995) is regarded as one of the most profound and practical spiritual leaders of the twentieth century. Born in Germany, Swami Radha moved to Canada after World War II, and traveled to India in the mid-1950s to meet her spiritual teacher, Swami Sivananda. Initiated into sanyas in 1956, she then returned to Canada and dedicated her life to interpreting the ancient wisdom of yoga for Western minds.

Swami Radha founded Yasodhara Ashram in 1963, now one of the longest running spiritual centres in North America. Her work continues in the devotional spirit in which it was created, maintaining the quality and integrity that were the essence of her life.

Swami Radha is a respected author of over ten books, several of which have become classics in the field of yoga, most notably *Kundalini Yoga for the West* and *Hatha Yoga: The Hidden Language*. Her published works represent a living legacy of yoga practice based on forty years of personal study and compassionate teaching.